What are the si

An ARIES is attracted to gemstones, steel,
and spices.

Silver and gold are great for a TAURUS.

GEMINI goes for geometrical shapes.

Heirlooms and keepsakes captivate a CANCER.

Take a LEO to Las Vegas.

A VIRGO is very fond of simple jewelry.

Color is important to a LIBRA.

A SCORPIO enjoys witty, humorous books.

A big bunch of flowers will suit a SAGITTARIUS.

A CAPRICORN likes to collect clocks.

Think unique when acquiring for an AQUARIUS.

A PISCES likes to plunge into water and music.

**These are just a few of the suggestions
you'll find in**
The Astrology Gift Guide!

The Astrology Gift Guide

Constance Stellas

A SIGNET BOOK

SIGNET
Published by New American Library, a division of
Penguin Putnam Inc., 375 Hudson Street,
New York, New York 10014, U.S.A.
Penguin Books Ltd, 80 Strand,
London WC2R 0RL, England
Penguin Books Australia Ltd, Ringwood,
Victoria, Australia
Penguin Books Canada Ltd, 10 Alcorn Avenue,
Toronto, Ontario, Canada M4V 3B2
Penguin Books (N.Z.) Ltd, 182–190 Wairau Road,
Auckland 10, New Zealand

Penguin Books Ltd, Registered Offices:
Harmondsworth, Middlesex, England

First published by Signet, an imprint of New American Library,
a division of Penguin Putnam Inc.

First Printing, October 2002
10 9 8 7 6 5 4 3 2 1

*To my father, whose gifts continue to bless me,
and to my husband, whose creative gifts
continue to amaze me.*

Acknowledgments

There are many people I would like to thank for helping me create this book. Karen Watts and Lark Productions gave support and encouragement as well as an introduction to the world of publishing. Joost Elffers, a devilish Scorpio, was instrumental in helping me clarify my ideas and advising me. His generosity led to a very fruitful relationship with my editor, Marie Timell. Thanks and appreciation go to both of them. Last, I'd like to thank my clients and friends who shared their stories of gifts and gift-giving with me.

Contents

Introduction	ix
Aries	1
Taurus	25
Gemini	49
Cancer	73
Leo	97
Virgo	121
Libra	145
Scorpio	169
Sagittarius	193
Capricorn	217
Aquarius	243
Pisces	267

Introduction

Have you ever faced Christmas, birthdays, or other gift-giving occasions without a clue as to what to buy for your family, friends, and associates? Meanwhile, do you know someone who seems to have the knack for always choosing the perfect gift? Selecting gifts that are meaningful is a special talent. But for most people, gift-giving is a bit hit or miss— sometimes our gift ideas are successful and sometimes they're not.

Often, despite our best and most loving intentions, finding the perfect gift can be constrained by our time limitations. Many people in Western society are overloaded with a variety of possibilities for gift choices. Searching out that ideal present can be time-consuming and frustrating. The holiday season, in particular, becomes a marathon of frantic shopping with no time to breathe and enjoy. At these times, it may feel like an impossible task to find meaningful gifts when there are so many people to give to, too many choices, and too little time. It is no wonder that the challenge of what to give someone can feel overwhelming!

There's a certain pressure to gift-giving as well, since gifts carry quite a bit of meaning. At best, a gift is a concrete way to reflect your thoughts and feelings about a person. A gift is also a way of expressing more than we can say out loud. For example, sometimes a gift tells us that a friendship is moving into a romance. At worst, receiving an ill thought out gift announces that a person doesn't really understand us at all. Any gift-giver's true aim is to give a gift that is meaningful and that makes someone happy. So what is the secret to finding a special gift, one that truly speaks to a person? We make people the happiest if we give them gifts that reflect our understanding of who they are and that accord with their natures. *The Astrology Gift Guide* is designed to increase your ability to give meaningful and well-chosen gifts, while reducing the amount of time you have to spend to do so. Because the guide offers fundamental insight into a person's character based on the ancient art of astrology, it enables you to pick the perfect gift for someone—one that will truly touch him or her where they live. If we look at gift-giving as an opportunity to give something that accords with a person's nature, in some small way we create a connection between the spiritual and material worlds. Why not select gifts that harmonize with a person's nature by surrounding the recipient with objects, colors, metals, and styles that contribute to his or her sense of well-being? Having insight into a person's character through his or her astrological sign can ensure that you always find the perfect gift.

Not only does *The Astrology Gift Guide* provide insight into character, it goes one step farther by providing hundreds of gift ideas based on astrological signs. Even if you don't fully understand astrology or someone's sign, you can still use this book. All you need to know is someone's birthday to discover dozens of creative ways to give to that person.

Astrology—or the planets' positions on a person's birthday and what that means—is the handiest and most profound way to know someone's character. An astrology chart is a personal, cosmic recipe that details all the ingredients that make up each person. The chart outlines our strengths and weaknesses and also what we do and don't enjoy. The ancient astrologers probably never imagined their observations could be used to help a person choose a gift. But, if you think about it, a gift reflects your understanding of the person to whom it is given. Astrology increases your understanding of a person's character and so can be immeasurably helpful in choosing gifts.

In order to help you select excellent and resonant gifts, I have described the twelve astrological signs, focusing on each sign's preferences. It is these preferences for different objects, scents, materials, styles, and colors that will determine whether a gift makes a sign happy or not. In my years of experience as a practicing astrologer, I always paid particular attention to my clients' likes and dislikes. I would carefully observe what they wore, any jewelry or gems they might possess, the decor of their homes and any special objects they treasured. Often my clients asked me for general information on what would please their loved ones. Soon people began to consult me for specific gift ideas. Though my suggestions might take into account different variables, such as the occasion, age, and sex of the person, at his or her core, my suggestions reflected ancient astrological references to the materials, scents, colors, and style preferences of different astrological signs. People responded well to this "new use" for astrology. I remember recommending gardening books and a finely woven dress or scarf to a man searching for a gift for his Virgo fiancée. It turned out that she was a landscape gardener and weaver! Astrology pointed me—and him—in exactly the right direction.

In *The Astrology Gift Guide*, I share with you what I have learned in hopes of taking a bit of the frustration out of gift-giving and perhaps saving you some time as well. If you have a pretty good idea of what you'd like to buy someone, often you can order it on-line! What could be simpler than that?

In the pages that follow, I describe the characteristics of each astrological sign, placing particular emphasis on the sign's likes and dislikes, to enable you to understand a sign's character well enough to choose a gift for someone. Throughout the text I offer gift suggestions and ideas. At the beginning of each sign I present a table outlining a sign's ancient associations, such as its ruling planet, colors and metal, gemstones, and part of the body the sign rules. In addition, I've included helpful information on a sign's ruling passion (Leo: to live in the spotlight), home style (Capricorn: classic and conservative) and underlying philosophy (Gemini: keep it interesting). The information provided in these tables serves as a tip-off to character while it prompts your creative juices to flow, causing you to generate a myriad of inspired gift ideas.

For those truly short on time and creativity, I've provided shopping lists of dozens of gift ideas at the end of every sign. These lists are divided according to sex, male and female, and are further divided according to price category: *Thrifty Saturn, Luxurious Venus,* and *Bountiful Jupiter.* In astrology, Saturn is the planet that rules limitations and constriction, so if your budget is temporarily constricted, look under *Thrifty Saturn.* Venus pertains to pleasure and luxury. If you are in a medium budget category, look for gift suggestions in *Luxurious Venus.* In astrology, Jupiter is called the "great benefic." This is the planet of exuberant excess. So, if the sky is the limit, look at *Bountiful Jupiter* suggestions. There is also a category for children and teens, though some suggestions for boys or girls might suit adults and vice versa.

In my discussion of the different signs, I also mention some well-known people of each, both to help illuminate the character of the sign and to provide gift ideas. Since we are most comfortable with those who share our signs, I suggest you keep these cultural figures in mind when buying gifts. For example, purchase a book by an author of the same sign as your friend. Give someone a video starring and directed by someone of the same sign. Perhaps even buy someone a work of art by a fellow sign member.

One last note: How a person receives a gift or responds to a gift-giving occasion is often different across the signs. For example, a Cancer's response to a gift might be awkward shyness. It takes Cancer people a while to get used to something, so often they show their pleasure later. In order to ensure your gift-giving success, I also offer descriptions of a sign's approach to *receiving* gifts for a variety of different holidays and celebrations, along with more gift suggestions based on the occasion. For example, marriage is an especially big event for Libra, so be sure to buy a significant wedding gift well ahead of time. Meanwhile, buying a new home is a primary event for Taurus. Don't forget that housewarming present!

As you read this book, you will begin to get a feel for all the signs and come to a new understanding of the many ways people express and enjoy themselves. You will begin to improvise your own gift selections based on your knowledge of the signs. Tuck *The Astrological Gift Guide* into your pocket or purse while shopping. With this book along, you will never again feel stumped by what gifts to get friends, family, business associates, or lovers. Instead, you will have the pleasure of giving pleasure to the people you care about.

—Constance Stellas

Aries
March 21–April 19

ARIES
A Cardinal Yang Sign

SYMBOL:	The Ram
RULING PLANET:	Mars
ELEMENT:	Fire
BODY PART:	Head and face
FAVORED POSSESSIONS:	Metal sculpture, caps, fireplaces, red sweater
COMMUNICATION STYLE:	Direct
HOME STYLE:	Bold and casual
COLORS AND METAL:	Red, spring green, iron
FOOD, PLANTS, FLOWERS:	Hot peppers, onion, thistle, holly, honeysuckle
PARTNERSHIP STYLE:	Ardent and fun-loving
RULING PASSION:	Desire to be first
PHILOSOPHY:	Charge ahead and see what happens
GEMSTONES:	Diamonds, malachite
WISHES OR GOALS:	To initiate enough projects to keep life vibrant
UNCONSCIOUS DESIRE:	To be comfortable following instead of leading
FOR GIFT-GIVING, KEEP IN MIND:	Aries likes gifts that inspire.

Character Traits and Symbols

Aries, the first sign of the zodiac, marks the beginning of spring. The vernal equinox also marks the beginning of the renewal holidays of Easter and Passover. The image of the ram or Paschal Lamb figures in both the Jewish and Christian traditions. And the ram, with those beautiful curled horns, is Aries' symbol. It is interesting to see how ancient holidays resonate with astrological symbols. The ram was identified with the Egyptian god Ammon, and in Greek mythology, Phrixus sacrificed to Zeus the ram that had saved him, and he gave the Golden Fleece to King Æetes. As a reward, Zeus placed the ram in the heavens as the constellation of Aries. The ram is interested in butting heads with life. There are some Aries who have become timid sheep but the spark of an idea or project that really interests them is enough to fan the flames and get them back to their fiery natures.

Each sign of the zodiac symbolizes a different part

of the soul's journey. Aries is the sign of birth and the starting point. Those born under Aries are learning how to express their individuality. Aries delights in the energy of doing and accomplishing. Beginnings and the sparks of ideas are all character traits of Aries.

Each sign of the zodiac has an element: fire, earth, air, or water. Aries' element, as you might imagine, is fire. The fire signs are all energetic and inspirational. They have wonderful hunches and the energy to carry them out. Aries' energy and impetuosity is the strongest of the zodiac. Leo and Sagittarius, the other two fire signs, may keep Aries company for a while, but Aries outpaces them by being the master and mistress of many pots simmering at once. The image of a volcano is a good one for these dynamic people. Their enthusiasm burns brightly and they are very impatient. Their goal in life is to get things moving. Aries is not bad-tempered. When they get angry they express their feelings and then it is over. These people rarely hold grudges because their enthusiasm just carries them to the next project.

Aries energy can also betoken a short attention span, which leads to many beginnings and few conclusions. Aries is like champagne: bubble, bubble, and then it goes flat. The challenge for Aries is to keep interested in whatever is going on long enough to complete the assignment or task. The best rhythm for Aries is to work on something with short bursts of concentration.

When considering gifts for this adventurous sign, think of gifts that are bold and bright and humorous. Aries loves to see things that make him laugh.

For example, the rooster is ruled by Aries. Consider giving your Aries a variety of china and painted dishware with a rooster motif—a reminder to strut. Ancient associations of a sign can also be creatively translated into modern gift ideas that are practical, meaningful, and resonant. For example, Aries, as a fire sign, is associated with Hephaestus, the ancient Greek god of fire and forge. Andirons for the fire, metal candle sticks in interesting shapes, and wrought iron are all gifts to salute Aries' connection with forging. Aries children may enjoy the very simple game of jacks. The jingle of the metal jacks combined with a bouncing red ball is pleasing to their eyes and ears. Aries likes distinct and rhythmic sounds.

In Roman mythology, Aries was called Mars, the god of war. Mars, the red planet, rules Aries. In keeping with this warlike ancestry, Aries also rules iron, weaponry, and surgery. While you may not want to give your spitfire Aries girlfriend an ancient saber or Winchester rifle, consider fencing lessons or skeet shooting. Aries men may not be any more interested in weapons than other people are, but they will appreciate fine carving knives, good cutlery, scissors, and may love to carry a pocketknife or Swiss army knife. In astrology, when we consider the best day for surgery we examine the position of Mars because it rules the knife.

The parts of the body associated with Aries are the head and face. You may notice that Aries people have very strong foreheads and sometimes eyebrows that arch in a manner suggestive of the ram's curled horns. Because the sign is linked with the head, Aries likes caps and hats although they do not usually wear them for warmth. Their strong and fiery metabolism keeps them warm in the winter even with a light coat. Though you might think the perfect gift for Aries would be a bicycle helmet, Aries will not want to wear it. They like the freedom of a bare head. You could even end up fighting with them over the need for the protection of a helmet as they tear around town or the countryside. Baseball caps, cowboy hats, and other jaunty head apparel suit Aries.

Aries likes to live anywhere they can get in and out of easily. Small, cluttered rooms make them feel claustrophobic. Urban Aries will want to live near a park or somewhere they can walk and think about their next project. Rural Aries will enjoy hiking for the same purpose.

Gifts that emphasize "me first" or "number one" are perfect for Aries. One Aries teacher I know always gives out "number one" stickers to her first-graders. I asked her how she got the idea and she said when she was a child her favorite teacher gave her a red "number one" to wear around her neck. She loved it and when she became a teacher she thought her students would like it too. Liking to be number one is not conceit. It's just that Aries have an almost childlike attitude that says, "I am here and happy to have you recognize me."

Aries prefer to be in their own business; they do not like to answer to anyone and bristle at taking orders. They can handle many projects at once but lack the ability to easily cooperate. They need to be the boss and to have employees answer to them. One Aries friend, a producer and artist, found a way to get an intern from a local college to help him with his work. He had no money to pay him and the intern basically ran around doing errands, but having an employee suited his self-image. The intern felt he was learning something valuable, so they made a good team.

A crucial business skill that Aries needs to cultivate is tact. These energetic people are so filled with delight at their ability to make things happen that they sometimes forget that others have their own viewpoint. If Aries feel someone does not appreciate their project or ideas they will walk away. This temperament is not effective in the long run.

Colors and Flowers

Colors for Aries are bright and vibrant. Red, crimson orange, and yellows usually suit these people and the vibrant color of spring green or the green of Granny Smith apples is also a good one to keep in mind when shopping for Aries. If you would like to give flowers to your Aries, consider red carnations and coxcombs. Multicolored Gerbera flowers would also be an attractive gift. Large, bold flowers are preferable to dainty blossoms. The beautiful bush firethorn is an Aries plant, as are cacti. Aries would enjoy all trees with thorns, such as holly.

Metals, Gems, and Materials

Aries' premier metal, as mentioned before, is iron. In addition to wrought iron, I have frequently noticed that Aries have a horseshoe above their doors.

For jewelry, yellow gold is preferable to silver or platinum. Red stones and gems resonate with Aries. The rulership of gems and signs has a long and complicated history and frequently there are a variety of gems linked with signs. Aries rules diamond cutters but diamonds are traditionally linked with Leo and Libra, as well as Aries. Garnets belong to Scorpio and Aries. If you imagine a child walking through the countryside and picking up a gleaming red rock or mineral, you will have a good picture of something that would appeal to your Aries. Rubies, with their rich red color, are a perfect adornment for Aries.

The most resonant material for Aries is sheepskin. A wooly sheepskin coat or vest would be a fine gift choice. A hand-knit sweater, preferably red, would be an excellent gift. Clothes for Aries should be durable and not cumbersome. These people are not apt to spend a lot of time taking care of their wardrobe, so a gift of clothing should be good-looking and require low maintenance.

Food, Herbs, Tastes, and Scents

All spices suit Aries. There may be a few of these fire natives who like plain boiled food, but I imagine they will at least add a lot of salt. If your Aries is a cook, consider a gift of exotic spices. Spices that are considered warming tastes, such as ginger, garlic, cayenne, pepper, and mustard, are all tastes Aries enjoy. The barbecue or open fire is a perfect place to find Aries men and women. Perhaps they feel like Hephaestus when they spread a fiery blend of spices on the London broil or spareribs. One Aries client of mine loved hot chili. The poor guy had an ulcer but he would not forgo his chili. He told me he drank milk to coat his stomach and then piled on the red hots. I hope his stomach held out.

I can't really recommend smoking cigarettes or cigars, but I have noticed that Aries people manage to smoke with enjoyment and without as many ill effects as others suffer. A box of fine cigars may be a present for Aries. Another way to indulge Aries would be with gifts of incense or scented candles. Pungent scents such as sage, sandalwood, or cedar would be favorites.

Travel

Traveling for Aries can be a spur-of-the-moment event. If Aries has the means, he will think nothing of popping over to England or traveling across the country for a weekend. Most Aries do not suffer greatly from jet lag and arrive at their destination ready to explore. Short trips are always a tonic and Aries will always appreciate practical travel gifts that make moving about easy. For air travel, Aries should remember to walk and stretch. Sitting for long periods of time cramps them. A good gift might be hand-held exercise balls to relieve the stress of being in a confined space. Britain is Aries-ruled, as are Denmark, Germany, and Palestine. It is interesting that, with the exception of Denmark, each of these countries has had a bellicose history.

Sports

Sports usually attract Aries because they have energy to burn. People in this sign are quite coordinated. Paddleball, or a punching bag (for men or women) will help work off energy. Aries have bursts of energy and can do very well in sports such as sprinting and track. Fencing and martial arts are also areas where Aries excels. I have also noticed that Arians are frequently very good dancers and have an affinity for tap. The rhythm of the tapping releases aggression and expresses their elegant, graceful side. Give gifts to your Aries that will keep their equipment in good shape. Red, orange, or yellow exercise wear would always be appreciated. Celebrities and sports figures who embody grace and power include Jennifer Capriati, Marilu Henner, and the marathon runner Ingrid Kristiansen. The great basketball player and commentator Walt Frazier is an Aries. In football, the Heisman Trophy winner Earl Campbell is also an Aries.

Intellectual and Artistic Interests

Aries is keenly aware of social injustices and is dedicated to helping a favored cause. They are always ready to take action on others' behalf and their fiery leadership can be a key ingredient in any organization or project. Al Gore is Aries. His blunt style did not endear him to many people, but it would have been interesting to see how his warrior side would have manifested if he had been elected. Aries get bored if life stays the same. I think this is why they enjoy working for personal as well as social change. Books about people who have radically changed their lives may be of great interest to Aries. *The Autobiography of Malcolm X* is an example; Malcolm X was a Taurus with an Aries moon.

Artistic projects are also good ways for Aries to keep life interesting. These people do not like a slow pace and enjoy having many irons in the fire. Metal sculpture and welding are unique hobbies that sometimes attract Aries. The sign has both visual and musical abilities if Aries can be patient enough to develop them. A set of drums for Aries could be the beginning of a great hobby and a way to express martial enthusiasm. The neighbors might not be happy but drumming could keep Aries in top form.

Romance

Impetuous Aries moves in and out of romance quickly. These people express their passion but it might not stay around too long. The good quality about Aries is that you will always know where you stand with them. These people are rarely deceitful. If you do hitch up with an Aries, romance will play a large part of your married life. Sparring and making up keeps things interesting as both Aries men and women like a bit of challenge in a relationship. Both the men and women pursue their lovers. When considering gifts for Aries in love, choose something that will encourage activity and adventure. A great gift would be tickets to a sporting event or a ticket for skydiving. If you have a fireplace in your home, this will be the scene of many romantic encounters.

Well-Known Aries

The list of well-known Aries artists is interesting. The sign has great leadership capacities and Aries are frequently found as directors of businesses or artistic projects. The film directors Francis Ford Coppola, Akira Kurosawa, Barry Levinson, and David Lean are all Aries. Warren Beatty, who is an actor and director, is also a Ram. A boxed set of all *The Godfather* (Coppola) movies and the DVD of *Lawrence of Arabia* (David Lean) are a couple gift possibilities for Aries.

When you consider Aries performers, it is a curious fact that three of the major stars of Hollywood's golden era were born on the same day. Spencer Tracy, Bette Davis, and Gregory Peck were all born on April 5. Their movies are classics. Mary Pickford, one of the founders of United Artists Studio, was also an Aries. She was a pioneer in giving actors a share of the movie theater ticket receipts. Each one of these performers was striking for the intensity and clarity of their work. Contemporary actresses Julie Christie, Ellen Barkin, and Reese Witherspoon are Aries.

Marlon Brando, whose explosive performances created a new standard for acting, is an Aries. His passionate work and his blasé attitude toward his own fame and accomplishments befit Aries impatience. He also used his fame to publicize issues regarding Native American rights. Contemporary Aries actors include Matthew Broderick and *Gladiator* star Russell Crowe. Biographies or copies of any of these actors' films would be interesting gifts for an Aries.

There are so many Aries musicians that they could

provide gift inspirations for years. The composers Henry Mancini, Elton John, Stephen Sondheim, and Andrew Lloyd Webber are all Aries. These men have created some of the most best-known popular music. Stephen Sondheim's musical *Sweeney Todd*, about the demon barber of Fleet Street, combines a dark story with incredibly sweet melodic music—a good description of Aries characteristics. Listen to the CD or take your Aries to a performance. In classical music the great prolific genius Johann Sebastian Bach was an Aries. The collected set of Bach's works features more than two hundred cantatas, many preludes and fugues, and twenty concerti. It would keep anyone interested for years. Sergei Rachmaninoff, a Russian composer who wrote wildly passionate piano music, and the Hungarian composer Béla Bartók were Aries.

Three great twentieth-century conductors—Toscanini, Stokowski, and Herbert von Karajan—were also Aries. If you gave a recording of Bach or Rachmaninoff by any of these conductors you would have an Aries doubleheader.

Two noteworthy Aries performers are Aretha Franklin and Diana Ross. Another contemporary singer who has soared in popularity is Celine Dion. Her fellow Aries performer is Mariah Carey. These ladies all have the force and drive that typifies Aries.

In literature, two outstanding playwrights of the twentieth century, Samuel Beckett and Tennessee Williams, were both Aries. Beckett created new, spare, mordantly funny plays, and Williams was the most lyrical, poetic playwright in recent history. The movie *A Streetcar Named Desire* was a collaboration between Tennessee Williams, Marlon Brando, and director Elia Kazan, two Aries and a Virgo. This is usually a tough, irritating combination, but together they created great art. Also, the poet Robert Frost was an Aries. The title of his poem "The Road Less Traveled" has come into the popular vocabulary. "The road less traveled" could be an Aries motto.

Aries: Response to Celebrations and Occasions

BIRTHDAY

The number one holiday for Aries is his or her birthday. Aries wants to be noticed and appreciated on that day and will have no hesitation in telling any- and everyone that this is when the world had the pleasure of receiving him or her. You may not have to hunt around for presents for your Aries. He or she will be quite forthcoming about likes and dislikes. I know one Aries man who sends a letter each year to his children with top picks for Christmas and birthday gifts. This is not conceit, just an efficient and direct way of ensuring that he'll receive what he would truly like to have.

CHRISTMAS/HANUKAH

This is a time of low energy for Aries. Winter is viewed as just a necessary evil for getting to spring and Aries need lots of warmth and color around this time of year. The festivities of the holidays may be more important than actual gifts, but you won't go wrong if you show your feelings to your Aries friend with a warm sweater or a holly wreath.

ENGAGEMENT/MARRIAGE

Getting married for Aries is more an occasion to party and less one of sentiment. What excites them about marriage is the idea that it is a new beginning. These people are not interested in getting weighed down with family traditions. Emphasize gifts that celebrate the Aries personality. If the bride or groom is interested in sports, tickets for a game or competition would be great.

NEW BABY

"New" is the operative word here and new Aries parents will enjoy the excitement of this addition to the family. Bright red mobiles or red baby clothes and rattles that make lots of noise would be perfect presents for this fire sign parent. Of course, a stuffed ram and a new sheepskin to lay the baby on will also make an Aries feel right at home.

ANNIVERSARY PRESENT

Since marriage is usually an exciting affair for Aries, an anniversary gift should reflect all the positive ardent feelings that brought you together in the first place. An Aries man will be pleased to receive sports equipment, CDs, or special gear that he needs to pursue his interests. The Aries woman would love to have a diamond tennis bracelet or some Austrian crystal that would flash on her wrist as she serves and volleys. Spending a lot of money is not terribly important to either Aries men or women. The key ingredient is that your present speaks to their individual image as dynamic partners.

MOTHER'S DAY

Don't be sentimental and give your Aries mother a corsage. Of course, because you are her child she'd be pleased but she'd be happier if you gave her a new golf club or tickets to a concert that she might never have a chance to get for herself. Cast iron cookery would be good *if* your mother likes to cook but an Aries who is exclusively a domestic sheep is rare.

FATHER'S DAY

Aries men are rough-and-tumble fathers who like to play with their kids. Sports gifts are good and some kind of adventure that you can do together is always a treat. Whatever business or profession your father is in, he would enjoy a gift that salutes his work and shows that as far as you are concerned he is number one. Try hats or baseball caps. Just don't buy him a tie! Aries dads aren't all that interested in dressing up.

GRADUATION

Aries has a pragmatic attitude toward learning. If the subject is interesting and your Aries understands the purpose for it, he can be a good student. If he is bored he will not apply himself at all. Consider a set of tools for either hobby use or equipment for the work or profession your Aries is beginning. Most Aries have an entrepreneurial streak. Books on starting a business or ways Aries could turn their favorite hobby into an occupation are good ideas.

VALENTINE'S DAY

Sentiment is not Aries' style, so they might not see the importance of this day. Luckily, red is one of Aries' favorite colors. For the Aries man, you might try a large red box of chocolate or a casual pullover. Turtlenecks are too confining. For the Aries woman you should definitely go for red roses. Sexual passion is ruled by Mars, so even if you forget to buy something, there are ways to express your ardor.

NEW HOME

Aries like space and plenty of room for play at home. Avoid small breakable tchotchkes. A door chime that plays reveille might be the perfect touch for a martial Aries. Also consider long fireplace matches. Aries loves to play with fireplaces and can get very excited about having all the necessary equipment to fan the flames.

THANK-YOU PRESENT

If you know your Aries well, consider giving a humorous present such as a T-shirt that says THANKS TO THE GREATEST. If you are giving a present to someone you do not know well, remember that Aries likes to be thanked but does not like to have a big fuss made about his or her generosity. Consider the jazz CD of a favorite composer, or a bottle of Scotch. Aries may be more partial to liquors than to wines.

ANYTIME PRESENT

The surprise will be half the fun of the present since Aries welcomes the new. Baseball caps, a mug with number one on it or an impromptu party or trip would suit this sign. A kit with all the fixings to make hot chili could be a big hit as well. A Superman bathrobe could be a great surprise for an Aries man.

Aries Gift Suggestions

ARIES MAN

Thrifty Saturn

Pepperoni pizza
Red baseball cap
Punching bag
Johann Sebastian Bach CDs
Barbecue tools
Gourmet coffees
Cigars
CDs by Aries pianist Murray Periah
Unusual Scotch
Dart board
A lighter

Luxurious Venus

Tennis racquet
Carving set
Patchouli scent
Fireplace tools
Wood carvings
Mahogany bookshelves
Cowboy hat
Sheepskin coat
Antique saber
Salsa CDs
Malachite paperweight
CD of *The 1812 Overture*

Bountiful Jupiter

Diamond cuff links
Grand piano
Ancient Corinthian columns
Ancient arrowheads
A flock of sheep
Etchings
Adventure tour
Antique rifles
A hunt club
Bagpipes
A conga line
Red Ferrari

ARIES WOMAN

Thrifty Saturn

A pepper wreath
Sword fern plants
Manicure set
Red hematite
Collection of red lipsticks
Fireplace matches
Gourmet pesto (basil)
Wool headband
Hatpins
Kohl eye makeup
Red silk teddy or panties

Luxurious Venus

Red wool shawl
Antique hatrack

Spice jars
Wrought iron candle sticks
China with rooster motif
Feng shui gong
Malachite jewelry
Flamenco dance lessons
Sheepskin rug
Unusual toaster
Monogrammed sheets

Bountiful Jupiter

Mahogany furniture
Trip throughout Italy
Portable barbecue
Cinnabar incense bottle
Chinese ginger jars
Big diamonds
Large landscape/pastoral paintings
Field of poppies
Scarlet pashmina shawl
Red Vespa
A kangaroo

ARIES BOYS AND TEENS

Erector set
Fire helmet
Superman comics
Toy fire engine
Magnets
A wolf model or stuffed animal
Baseball caps
A slingshot

Orange shirts
Toboggan
Motorcycle jacket
Pirate costume
Gladiator costume
Fencing equipment
Dart board
Punching bag
Military medals
Book of firsts
CDs by the Rolling Stones
Bongo drums
Steel drums
Skull ring
Wood carving set
The Avengers (video series)
Motorcycle jacket
Red sweater

ARIES GIRLS AND TEENS

Castanets
Red baseball cap
Ice skates
Wooly stuffed toy sheep
Croquet set
Monogrammed duffel bag
Garnet ring
Spring green cotton jacket
Ladybug bag
Rose quartz
Red scooter
A baby lamb (or a stuffed lamb)

Tap shoes
Red lipstick
Henna body art
Eyebrow piercing
Snow globe
Black glycerin soap
Red leather jacket
Stop watch
Jeweled barrettes
Mahogany jewelry box
Red jasper
Tennis racquet
Sheepskin vest
Hiking boots
Diamond earrings

Taurus
April 20–May 20

TAURUS
A Fixed Yin Sign

SYMBOL:	The Bull
RULING PLANET:	Venus
ELEMENT:	Earth
BODY PART:	Throat, neck, thyroid gland
FAVORED POSSESSIONS:	A piggy bank, real estate, soft scarves
COMMUNICATION STYLE:	Deliberate
HOME STYLE:	Comfy and relaxing
COLORS AND METALS:	Pale Turquoise and pink, copper, bronze
FOOD, PLANTS, FLOWERS:	Spearmint, berries, daisy, fig trees, cypress
PARTNERSHIP STYLE:	Steady and sensual
RULING PASSION:	Desire to be secure
PHILOSOPHY:	Touch conveys more than words.
GEMSTONES:	Clear green emerald
WISHES OR GOALS:	To create an economically safe and comfortable world
UNCONSCIOUS DESIRE:	To possess everything
FOR GIFT-GIVING, KEEP IN MIND:	Taurus likes gifts of value that last.

Character Traits and Symbols

Taurus, the second sign of the zodiac, is a fixed sign. Taurus is located solidly in the middle of its season, spring. In astrology, the fixed signs are the powerhouses of the zodiac. "Fixed" is also a good word to describe the definitiveness and stubbornness that is intrinsic to the sign.

The earth is Taurus' element, and giving and receiving material goods play an important part in Taurus' character. These people like things and will always appreciate your efforts to choose a gift that speaks to them. A Taurus is not always materialistic but his or her domain is the tangible world. Taurus feels grounded in the five senses, especially the sense of touch. They are usually collectors and keep everything that is given to them. Taurus can be immovable in his or her habits. If you find a gift that works consider giving a variation of it every year. Taurus won't mind consistency.

The Taurus symbol is the bull. The symbol for this

sign used in astrology represents the head and horns of a bull. In ancient times the beginning of Taurus was celebrated as a feast of Maia (similar to our May Day), with the sun represented by a white bull with a golden disc between the horns, followed by a procession of virgins, who exemplified the fecundity of nature in the spring. A secondary myth for Taurus is that of Europa and Zeus. In mythology, Europa had a dream that two continents were trying to possess her. Asia had given her birth and the other continent was as yet nameless. Zeus, looking down from Olympus, desired Europa, and to escape the watchful eye of his wife, Hera, he turned himself into a beautiful bull and spirited Europa away to the island of Crete. As they flew over the sea, the sea became land and the continent we know today as Europe was formed. Both ancient references speak to Taurus' love of land and nature. The bull is a symbol of rich, fertile power.

Most times the bull is placid and steady, but when provoked Taurus can be fiercely angry. You may never see a Taurus explosion of anger, but when it happens, it's a doozy. People get used to the normally quiet, easygoing demeanor of Taurus and are surprised when something provokes them into a blind fury. A Taurus who has had a blowout will also hold a grudge and it can take a good deal of effort to persuade him to be friendly again. Normally, however, Taurus is loyal and will stick with friends and family through thick and thin. Taurus will also not get involved with complicated feelings and psychological issues. You are either friend or foe and Taurus will make it clear which category a person is in.

The planet Venus is Taurus' ruler and it controls all luxuries. Venus also reigns over Libra but Libra is an air sign. Venus, ruling a sturdy earth sign, gives Taurus a sense of loving beauty for the way it feels. Taurus likes to touch materials, people, trees—really anything. The way something feels communicates directly to them. When I visit a museum with my Taurus friend I notice that he has to restrain himself from touching the contours of a statue or running his hand over the surface of a beautiful inlaid table.

Taurus' sensuality extends to food and sex. Taurus is lusty and very interested. Good food may be the prelude to a hot and heavy evening. Massage oils, soft towels, and peaceful music transport Taurus into a comfortable world. The sense of smell is highlighted in Taurus. I know a number of Tauruses who are "noses;" they actually create perfumes and are trained to detect subtle scents. Aromatherapy was designed for Taurus. Indeed, unpleasant smells can physically upset them.

Taurus at home wants ease and comfort. They are collectors and can create cheerful clutter in their space. When Taurus are about to make a change, they frequently purge everything and start from scratch. Taurus usually like to move things around so psychological or emotional changes can occur. In cities, Taurus prefers to be closer to the ground than up high. They like to keep their feet on the ground. It would be unusual for a Taurus not to own a home. Many people born under this sign are very good real estate investors and can do real estate deals on the side. If your Taurus is searching for a new occupation, consider giving him or her a book on real estate.

The throat, neck, and ears are the areas of the body ruled by Taurus. You may notice that many Tauruses have very thick, strong necks and very small ears. Tauruses need to protect the neck as they are vulnerable there. Wearing a scarf or muffler throughout the winter will keep the neck warm. Tauruses usually have robust health but their ears get cold quickly. A great gift would be ear muffs.

All the earth signs—Taurus, Virgo, and Capricorn—are at base very practical. They think concretely about life and managing their physical world of possessions, and the ability to handle money well is innate. It does not mean that all earth signs are wealthy, but they feel at home dealing with day-to-day reality. Their feelings are manifested by providing well for themselves and others. They do not tend to gush, as the water signs do, or get lost in airy thoughts, as the air signs do, or burn with enthusiasm, as the fire signs do. Taurus, in particular, knows how to get things done. Even if the person is not particularly successful, his advice will always be doable and considerate. If you are ever starting a business you may want to go over your plans with a Taurus and hear what he has to say.

Colors and Flowers

A matador flashes the red side of his cape to provoke the bull. Avoid red! The color is too hot for Taurus. Consider a peachy orange or tangerine. Taurus also likes turquoise and some pinks, as well as lavender. Usually Taurus prefers pastel tones to shocking colors. If you imagine the budding cherry blossoms of spring, you will have a good idea of the delicacy and strength of this sign. All products of the earth and flowers vibrate in accord with Taurus' nature. Many times, these people have gardens and grow their own vegetables. Daisies, columbine, daffodils, and larkspur are Taurus flowers, but there are very few varieties that Taurus will not enjoy. As with clothes, select flowers in pastel hues. Lilies of all types belong to Taurus. I always think of Taurus when the yellow lilies begin to bloom in the spring. An excellent present for an urban Taurus is a trip to a garden or the country. All fruit trees are Venus-ruled. Taurus would enjoy pomegranate, ash, cypress, and pecan trees. One Taurus friend always brings a sack of pecans to me each time he returns from "down South."

Metals, Gems, and Materials

Copper and brass belong to both Libra and Taurus because both are ruled by Venus. However, a complete set of copper cookware may be an ideal gift for Taurus especially. If your Taurus is not particularly domestic, consider a copper-topped table or brass dishes as decorative items. Taurus likes jewelry, and both men and women may have collections of rings and necklaces. Emeralds belong to Taurus. I have wondered since piercing has become a fashion if Taureans have more nose rings than other signs. Alabaster and moss agate are other semiprecious stones that appeal to Taurus. Jade is associated with Libra as well as Taurus as both are ruled by Venus. Very light green jade jewelry or carvings would suit Taurus perfectly. I know one Taurus who never wore jewelry but decided the only thing she wanted from her mother's estate was a jade necklace and earrings.

Taurus enjoys both silver and gold and will appreciate rare metals such as platinum. When you consider buying jewelry for Taurus be mindful of value. Taurus has a heightened sensitivity for real value in things and would prefer a real gem that is smaller and well cut than a flashy piece of costume jewelry.

Taurus' style is easy and uncomplicated. Clothing must be comfortable to them; in fact, if it isn't, Taurus will do something unusual like throw something out. Both men and women like very soft fabrics and fuzzy-feeling material. Although leather is ruled by Saturn and belongs to Capricorn's sign, Taurus likes the feel of very soft leather or suede. Chamois cloth is an ideal texture.

Food, Herbs, Tastes, and Scents

Taurus loves taste and good food. Some Taureans have weight problems but others are rail thin and can freely indulge their love of good food. Whether their love is doughnuts or crepes Suzette, tasty sweets and gourmet specialties are usually a good gift choice. Avoid salty, fishy foods, such as kippers or tinned oysters. In general, Taurus tends to enjoy meat and is not partial to fish. The earth is his terrain, not the sea. I would think that a perfect Taurus gift would be a delivery of a different food specialty item each month. A fruit basket or box of cookies arriving each month suits Taurus' notion of consistency and the food will be thoroughly enjoyed. Master chef James Beard, who introduced the art of bread-making and many new dishes to the American public, was a Taurus. A perfect present might be a copy of his cookbook accompanied by a basket of fresh breads. There are also specialty beef houses that send filet mignon or sides of beef in a special refrigerated pack. This would be a great gift.

Spices and herbs for Taurus tend to be sweet. Licorice, peppermint, and curry would all please Taurus' palate. Taurus has an excellent sense of smell and enjoys rich, sweet scents. A little vanilla extract behind the ears would remind Taurus of the warm smell of baking cookies and keep him or her happy for hours. Other possibilities are jonquil and almond scents.

Travel

Travel may require some effort for Taurus. They like being in different places but not necessarily getting there. One Taurus lady I know always brings her pillows from home when she travels. She needs the familiar feel when she goes to sleep. Travel by car may be Taurus' preferred style. Ireland is a Taurus-ruled land and the green of the Emerald Isle is an image that probably would relax any stressed-out Taurus. Northern Holland is also Taurus-ruled. Visiting rows of tulips would be a wonderful experience for nature-loving Taureans. Other places that resonate with Taurus are Poland, Mantua, and Parma, Italy. Parma may be a favorite for Taurus. It is the home of the delicious cured meat, prosciutto, and the entire city has the scent of this delicacy. In the U.S., St. Louis is considered a Taurus city. Travel gifts could include secure money belts and an aromatic spritzer for the plane.

Sports

Taurus may not be the most sports-minded sign. There is a sensual laziness about some of them that encourages sitting and dreaming rather than huffing and puffing. Imagine Ferdinand the Bull lying in the pasture contemplating a flower. Taurus does enjoy hiking in the woods, some racquet sports, and cross-country skiing. They are good at team sports. Gear for yoga class or a gentle martial art such as aikido or t'ai chi would be a great gift. Yoga tapes or music to stretch by would also fit the bill. Taurus has great stamina and if they establish a workout routine when they are young, they will stick to it all their lives. One Taurus client walked 100 blocks every other day come rain or shine. On the opposite days he lifted weights. He kept this schedule up well into his seventies. Taureans often have powerful physiques and enjoy weight lifting. The champions Sugar Ray Robinson and Joe Louis were both Taurus. Other well-known Taureans are Andre Agassi, in tennis, and in baseball, Reggie Jackson and the great legend Willie Mays.

Intellectual and Artistic Interests

Taurus is not particularly interested in theoretical ideas. People born under this sign want to know how

thoughts can tangibly improve their own or others'
living conditions. They love reading history and fiction. They usually have a sense of ease about life and
faith and harmony in the universe.

Artistic interests for Taurus usually concern music.
When I ask if they sing, almost every person I see
who is a Taurus or has Taurus prominently in their
chart says "Oh, I love to sing but I have a terrible
voice." All Tauruses who believe they have terrible
voices should investigate this limiting idea and at
least sing in the shower. They may be surprised at
the results if they study singing or at least practice
themselves. Humming is also a great way to relieve
stress. CDs of classical, jazz, or pop tunes will keep
a melody in your Taurus' heart.

Another possible artistic outlet is dance. Taurus
may enjoy taking ballet or modern dance or just
going to a club and letting it all hang out.

Romance

Taurus is not a flashy romantic but the upside is
that the people in this sign are never fickle. Both
Taurus men and women may be slow to commit but
they will remain true. They never chase after romance but expect it to come to them. Similar to their
opposite sign, Scorpio, people born under Taurus
have a strong sex drive. Get out those Victoria's Secret catalogues and have a field day! Taurus may not
flaunt their feelings but the passion and vigor are
there. In romantic encounters, the sense of touch is
very important for Taurus. Almond scented massage
oils and a velvet or fur glove for special rubs would

make any Taurean feel cherished. Going off for a romantic weekend or getaway in the country will also encourage Taurus' romantic side.

Well-Known Taureans

Many singers have Taurus prominently placed in their astrology charts. The greatest crooner of all, Bing Crosby, was a Taurus. Bing embodied a relaxed ease that is the hallmark of a balanced Taurus. Perhaps the most prolific American songwriter of all time, Irving Berlin, was also a Taurus. He had incredible stamina and lived till his late nineties. The Taurus team of Bing Crosby singing Berlin's song "White Christmas" has defined Christmas for years. If your Taurus enjoys a bit of kitsch, he/she may get a kick out of recordings or the televised performances of Liberace. The music is fine and the costumes are a dream. Other musicians are Burt Bacharach, Bobby Darin, Barbra Streisand, and Ella Fitzgerald. A noteworthy contemporary Taurus singer is one of the fabulously talented Jackson family, Janet Jackson.

Classical music lovers may feel in tune with the great composer Johannes Brahms. His waltzes in particular have a sensual order that resonates for Taurus. Peter Tchaikovsky was also born under Taurus. His ballet music for the *Nutcracker Suite* and *Swan Lake* is so memorable that almost everyone knows a few of the melodies. A more recent composer, Erik Satie, was Taurus. Three piano pieces of his called the "Gymnopedie" are extraordinarily beautiful and calming. Buy a recording of these pieces and you and your Taurus will immediately feel soothed.

The creator of modern dance, Martha Graham, was a Taurus, as was one of the prima ballerinas of the past century, Margot Fonteyn.

Taurus likes to think big. Two of the greatest geniuses in history, Shakespeare and Leonardo da Vinci, were born under Taurus. Both of these artists produced an incredible body of work. And their biographies seem to say that both artists were very concerned with the practical aspects of making a living. Taurus is not likely to forget about paying the rent. There are numerous biographies of Shakespeare, copies of his plays, and sonnets that would be excellent gifts for your Taurus. Da Vinci's prints, paintings, writings, sketches, inventions, and sculptures are all available in reproduction. Taurus likes beautiful coffee table books. It doesn't matter if the book is expensive as long as it has beautiful photographs and is artistically laid out and well printed.

In film, David O. Selznick, producer of *Gone with the Wind*, and Orson Welles were Taurus, as are performers Jack Nicholson and Al Pacino. Take a look at Pacino's controlled, measured performance in *The Godfather*. In Taurus fashion, when he blows up, he is so violent he rattles the scenery. If you consider each of these artists, there is a very definite and grounded quality about each of them.

Taurean comedians have made a contribution to all of us. Carol Burnett is one of the funniest comediennes in showbiz. Two other very funny Taureans are Jay Leno and Jerry Seinfeld. These guys are also very good business people. Taurus may be more likely to spend their money on luxury items rather than just watching it grow.

Actresses born under Taurus are a fascinating group. The most famous is Katharine Hepburn. Katharine Hepburn contradicts the notion that Taurus is not good at sports. She was a sportswoman in many of her movies. She was also very mindful of her value as a star. She knew she wanted to be a star and that she had that "something" to achieve it. Her autobiography is aptly named, *Me.* Other wonderful Taurean actresses are Shirley MacLaine, Ann-Margret, Michelle Pfeiffer, Barbra Streisand, Renée Zellweger, and Sheena Easton. Streisand is also a powerful singer and her CDs would make a lovely gift. Shirley MacLaine's books about her explorations into spiritual realms are very interesting because she brings a sense of practical inquiry to her experiences that is very centered.

Taurus: Response to Celebrations and Occasions

BIRTHDAY

Taureans like to feel cozy and comfortable on their birthdays. Whatever your Taurus considers a luxury is the exact thing to give. Even if you decide to celebrate with a special dinner or theater tickets, your Taurus will appreciate an actual present that he/she can keep to remember: "This is what I got for my such and such birthday." Chances are that every year is marked in the memory of Taurus by the gift that especially mattered. It is important to plan how you celebrate with Taurus; they like to know in advance what is going to happen. Surprise parties may not be a good idea.

CHRISTMAS/HANUKAH

The winter is a harmonious time for Taurus and most natives of this sign won't mind at all the shopping and preparations for the holiday. They will love assembling presents for family and friends. Holiday presents can be a blend of the practical and luxurious. If your Taurean man needs socks, he won't mind a bit to see his stocking stuffed with them, and if you really want to please him, make them cashmere. The key ingredient to pleasing a Taurus at holiday times is that the gift be of good quality. Fine liqueurs, fruit baskets, or roast chestnuts are all good holiday gifts.

ENGAGEMENT/MARRIAGE

Some Taureans may view marriage more like a corporate merger. The sign is romantic and affectionate but there is also a keen appreciation of the financial ramifications of a union between two people. Fine china, linens, silver, and traditional furnishings mean home to Taurus and both the men and women will appreciate more traditional gifts that commemorate the setting up of a new household. Also, Taurus won't mind duplicate gifts; after all, it is always handy to have a spare set of dishes.

NEW BABY

A child is a happy asset to Taurus' family life. Though some financial worries may beset a Taurus parent, Taurus' deep connection to nature and the earth makes a child a welcome and expected part of family life. Opening a savings account for the new baby would suit Taurus' sense of security. If the new baby is a Taurus, make sure your gifts are all sturdy, since Taurus babies, toddlers, and children are all quite strong and so hard on toys and furniture. Taurus children are very strong-willed; they do not like to do anything they are not ready to do. Cuddling and sweetness will succeed best with them, whereas giving orders will backfire.

ANNIVERSARY

This could be a quiet affair between husband and wife that ends up with soaking in the Jacuzzi or bathtub together. Gifts that are luxurious but practical are the most appreciated. Taurus values the steadiness and sensuality of a long marriage and is open to marking the occasion in a special way. A quiet but extravagant dinner may be called for here. As for gifts, Taurus wives won't mind variations on a theme for their anniversary. For example, a different piece of jewelry every year would be something to look forward to. Taurus husbands may consider additions to their fishing gear, art collection, or gardening equipment perfect gifts to mark a long marriage. Taurus husbands will also enjoy a leather portfolio or wallet to keep track of investments or spare cash.

VALENTINE'S DAY

The day for lovers brings out Taurus' sensual side, so here is a sign that is open to all the traditions of Valentine's Day. Flowers are expected (Thrifty Taurus will especially appreciate that you had to pay a premium). Romance is a priority for Taurus and their sense of touch is highly developed. If you want to give clothes, make sure the fabrics are very soft and in light colors. Chocolate in abundance will be sure to please. Both women and men love good scents. Bath oils, aromatherapy candles, or aftershave are all perfect gifts. Taurus is a bighearted sign and won't mind getting a schmaltzy Valentine.

MOTHER'S DAY

Mother's Day falls in Taurus' month, May, so many Taurus moms get a "twofer." Emphasize flowers for the garden or an arrangement of cut lilies for the home. A Taurus mother wants to feel that the material care she gives her family is reciprocated on Mother's Day. She may want someone to cook for her or to be taken out to a restaurant. A drive or hike in the country would also be a good idea.

FATHER'S DAY

Taurus dads may most appreciate time out from work and permission to relax for the day. Your gift to him should reinforce his notion of himself as the good provider and friend. Taurus dads like comfort. Give him a pillow for his special reclining chair. Soft sweaters, fine foods, gardening tools, or music may be just the toys that this steady and caring dad would enjoy. Books on investing and money management are apt to be a success. Many Taureans collect coins and may appreciate an addition to their collection.

GRADUATION

Most Taureans will have a good idea of what they want to do with their future. Graduation marks their entry into the job market and practical Taurus is usually prepared. Those who choose an artistic life may be very clever holding down secondary jobs to help keep them afloat until success comes. A gift that encourages them in making their dreams concrete will be most appreciated. The sign can be artistic and will appreciate a special piece of art, such as a paperweight with the school emblem or monogrammed glassware. A job offer after graduation would probably be the best present for a Taurus.

NEW HOME

Here is where you can go all out. Real estate is very important to Taureans as is filling their home chock-full of everything they love. They will never forget a well-chosen housewarming gift. Make it comfortable, classic, and circular. Taurus doesn't like sharp angles or outré designs. A vase, bowl, yellow roses, or sweets are sure to be winners. A gift basket of gourmet items would always be welcome. Because Taurus both loves his home and views it as an investment, he will want to improve it. These people usually are fixer-uppers. You might consider a gift subscription from Home Depot or another home oriented store.

THANK-YOU GIFT

If you know your Taurus well, give a teddy bear with a little balloon saying, "Thanks." Taureans like to be appreciated not only for what they do but like to know they have the affection of their friends and coworkers. Taurus is rather modest when it comes to being appreciated. A thank-you note might seem cold, but flowers, a show of affection, such as a big hug, or a small memento would mean a lot.

ANYTIME GIFT

If you say to your Taurus friend or spouse: "I was in Macy's the other day and I saw this waffle iron and thought of you, so I got it," you will give two-fold pleasure to him or her. The actual gift is important but keeping Taurus' likes and dislikes in your mind and acting on them is almost as important. Don't be afraid to pick up something silly or even tacky. Taurus likes to collect the things people give to them.

Taurus Gift Suggestions

TAURUS MAN

Thrifty Saturn

Money clip
CDs by Perry Como
Leather checkbook cover
Golf balls
Pecan candy
Beer keg
Books on investing
Books on real estate
Daffodil bulbs
Handkerchiefs
Software for budgeting

Luxurious Venus

Copper cookware
Alpaca sports jacket
Brown leather belt
Golf clubs
Beige silk or 100% cotton shirts
A comfortable lounging chair
CDs by Barbra Streisand
Sweet-smelling cologne
Trip to Leipzig, Germany
Set of liqueurs
Weightlifting equipment
Flannel sheets

Bountiful Jupiter

Kobe steaks or filet mignon
Home media system
Venture capital
Cowskin rug
Library of videos
Emerald ring or cuff links
Cherry wood cabinets
A farm
Fur ear muffs
A jeep
Truffles
A herd of cattle
Leather luggage
Oriental carpets
Home on the Isle of Rhodes

TAURUS WOMAN

Thrifty Saturn

Gardenia perfume
Lilies
Star anise spice
Ear clips
An Easter bonnet
Creamy yellow blouse (in silk or 100% cotton)
Ivy
Aromatherapy atomizer
Turquoise scarf
Cherry brandy
Larkspur flowers
Decorative tassels

Luxurious Venus

Shantung silk dress
Carved petrified wood
Alabaster bowl
Wall-to-wall carpeting
Copper-top table
Copper cookware
Poet's shirt (silk)
A yellow comforter
Truffles
Marzipan
Pink coral necklace
Coin bracelet or ring
Scarab necklace

Bountiful Jupiter

Limitless emeralds
Chanel No. 5
Antique wardrobe
A harp serenade
A butler
Acres of land
A casino
A personal banker
Satin sheets
Fluffy dogs
A rose garden
Many homes

TAURUS BOYS AND TEENS

A wallet
Stuffed toy bears

Maracas
Shares of stock
Karaoke set
Indoor sandbox
Yellow sweater
Toy cash register
Nose ring
Clarinet
Turquoise shirt
Cash
Irish music
Singing lessons
Copper earring
Trip to St. Louis
Guitar
Earphones
Brightly colored balls
Dune buggy
Leather backpack
Surround sound TV
White wall to paint on
Cookbook for kids
Coin collection
Cake
Savings account
Modeling clay

TAURUS GIRLS AND TEENS

Stuffed cow
Satin shoes
Pink purse
Turquoise wallet

Daisy appliqués
Musical jewel box
Mother Goose books
A garden house
Velvet hats
Leather purse
A hammock
Jade power bracelets
Bullseye
Silk throw pillows
Piggy bank
Yellow scarf
Singing lessons
Copper bracelet
Clown costume
SUV
Parakeet
Emerald post earrings
Makeup kit
Vanilla soap
Pressed flowers
Chocolate-covered cherries

Gemini
May 21–June 20

GEMINI
A Mutable Yang Sign

SYMBOL:	The Twins
RULING PLANET:	Mercury
ELEMENT:	Air
BODY PART:	Shoulders, hands, lungs
FAVORED POSSESSIONS:	A ceiling fan, pens and pencils, books/magazines
COMMUNICATION STYLE:	Talkative and witty
HOME STYLE:	Airy and uncluttered
COLORS AND METAL:	Light blue, light yellow, mercury
FOOD, PLANTS, FLOWERS:	Caraway, nuts, myrtle, lily of the valley, chestnut trees
PARTNERSHIP STYLE:	Charming and changeable
RULING PASSION:	Desire to gather and communicate ideas
PHILOSOPHY:	Two is better than one
GEMSTONES:	Blue zircon, aquamarine
WISHES OR GOALS:	To keep life and the world interesting
UNCONSCIOUS DESIRE:	That thoughts could become reality immediately
FOR GIFT-GIVING, KEEP IN MIND:	Gemini likes gifts that are varied and fun.

♊

Character Traits and Symbols

Gemini's dual nature comes from the sign's extraordinary mental facility and flexibility. One legend relates that, Gemini's symbol—the Twins, one mortal and one immortal—represents the brothers Castor and Pollux. Castor was mortal and Pollux immortal. When Castor met an untimely death, Pollux was inconsolable. Zeus pitied Pollux's grief and allowed him to live with his brother for six months of the year in the underworld. Another legend states that the two brothers never meet because when one brother is in heaven the other is on earth. The first legend expresses Gemini's desire for unity and the second expresses the separative impulse that also is native to Gemini. Gemini is fundamentally concerned with duality and their lifelong goal is to make peace with their opposing tendencies. You can understand now why Gemini has the reputation for going in two directions at once.

Gemini is ruled by Mercury—or Hermes, in Greek

mythology. There is a very popular Greek statue of Mercury that is now used as a symbol by messenger companies and FTD florists. Mercury wears a low-crowned hat with wings, on his feet are winged sandals, and he carries a wand, the caduceus. Mercury was Zeus' messenger. The caduceus, a wand with two entwined serpents and wings at the top, is the symbol of the medical profession. The serpent, Scorpio's symbol, represents life's healing energies and the wings at the top represent the messenger or physician who communicates the best ways of restoring health. Mercury, in ancient times, was also the god of commerce and the market. Gemini frequently work as go-betweens or agents for commercial transactions. Selling and working on commission are easy for them because they have good intuition on how to make connections with people.

Air, which symbolizes the realm of ideas, is their element. Like a butterfly, Gemini can flit from one idea to another. People born under Gemini can usually mimic other people, or mentally experiment with a half dozen theories at the same time. Gemini thrives on ideas and their transmission. They are born salespeople, generally optimistic and very good company. Gemini rarely broods because they do not pay attention to any one thought or feeling long enough to be sad. This is not always superficiality, merely Gemini's ruler, Mercury, the messenger god, saying, "Let's get on with it. There are hundreds of things to learn and experience."

Geminis also have great facility with language. Many of these people speak foreign languages and usually have excellent accents in all of them. A Gemini friend teaches dialects and has such a keen ear that he can imitate any accent. He was hired as a part-time detective because he could assume so many different voices. You will also notice when Geminis speak, regardless of their accent or speech pattern, their voices are very clear and they like the sound of words. Yes, they also like to talk. A great present would be a phone card!

When choosing gifts for Gemini, consider all modes and manners of communication. Gemini might be interested in calligraphy, shorthand, Morse code, walkie-talkies, or cell phones. A set of colored pencils, a bamboo pen, and special hand-blended inks are all Gemini gifts that would add glamour and fun to your Gemini's life.

I think it may have been a Gemini who designed a kaleidoscope. The ever-changing pictures and infinite patterns are as complex and entertaining as Gemini's brains and interests. Learning to focus the mind and clarify their thinking is a lifelong challenge for Gemini. Gifts that have a changeable nature like snow globes, kaleidoscopes, or crystal prisms entrance Gemini. The sign is often fond of interesting shapes and anything that is two-sided, two-faced, or reversible. A client of mine was a clockmaker and proudly showed me his beautiful watch with two separate faces and dials to accommodate two time zones. He was mystified how I could tell he was a Gemini!

Gemini rules the lungs and respiratory system. It is very important for Gemini to breathe well, as they tend to hold their breath when tense, thereby creating more tension. Allergies and even asthma can develop after years of tense breathing patterns. A

Gemini friend and healer developed a very simple therapy, which he called Breathing Coordination. After working as a choral director and learning how to produce a resonant tone by correct breathing, he observed that the diaphragm can become locked in a tense breathing pattern and this tension affects every other part of the body. His solution, simply put, was to emphasize the exhale and a good and deep inhale will follow. Try it the next time you are upset. Exhale completely and feel the natural good deep breath that comes next. If you do this three times successively, you can decrease stress immediately.

Gemini also rules the hands. If you observe a Gemini's hands, they are usually slender, well-formed, and very expressive. Gemini people speak with their hands a great deal and fidget with them when they are not talking. Specialty gloves of all kinds would delight this sign.

I often wonder if statistically there are more Gemini than other signs in high-rise buildings. High airy apartments with lots of windows are very attractive to Gemini. To balance the air element it is a good idea for Gemini to put rocks or houseplants in each of the four corners of their space. Gemini need to ground their tendency to get mentally carried away. Ceiling fans are a great addition to Gemini homes even if they do not live in a warm climate. The feeling of moving air is soothing to them.

Gemini needs constant change to fend off boredom. Avoid giving the same gifts year after year or you may find you do not have a Gemini friend. This very variable sign appreciates presents as offbeat as a Lithuanian/English dictionary or a pen pal in Zaire. A complete set of Gilbert and Sullivan's operettas would appeal to many Gemini men. The combination of the clever lyrics and beautiful melodies appeal to both mind and feelings. If your Gemini is a good mimic you might consider recordings or CDs of different accents and languages, language learning tapes, or a collection of sound effects. Gemini loves different sounds and would also respond well to environmental recordings. Consider a membership to a museum or concert series as a special gift for Gemini. These people like to get out and see what's going on. Puzzles and games that provide mental focus are stimulating and focusing. One Gemini I know learns another language every few years. He also teaches himself. This kind of curiosity is typically Gemini.

I know quite a few Gemini kids who have lots of trouble concentrating and their parents thought they had an attention deficit problem. I thought to myself, "I don't think that is their problem. They are just Gemini." The sign has a short attention span and must move around when they work or study. If schools put in standing desks they might find that some kids (especially Gemini) could concentrate better. It is also important that kids do not have the TV or radio on when they read. The buzz is comforting but these children need to hone their skills to concentrate on the task at hand. Their own nervous systems have enough to handle without reacting to more stimuli.

Colors and Flowers

The preferred color scheme for Gemini tends to silver, light green, white, light blue, and light yellow. Vibrant colors weigh these airy people down. All two-toned clothes would be great gifts for Gemini. Usually a mixture of white and a light color is appealing. A particular Gemini flower is lily of the valley. Airy ferns and wispy houseplants such as strawberry begonia or a spider plant with many "babies" are Gemini favorites also. Other Gemini flowers are baby's breath and azaleas. The mulberry tree is ruled by Gemini. In addition to being beautiful, mulberry trees are great to sit under and chat.

Metals, Gems, and Materials

Gemini's metal is quicksilver or mercury; however, it is not a good idea to do anything with this metal except watch it in a thermometer. But it does mean that Gemini usually prefer silver to gold and delicate filigree work suits the Gemini nature more than heavily carved silver pieces. The blue aquamarine is a perfect gem for Gemini. Striped stones, beryl, and blue zircons also resonate with Gemini. Clear quartz crystal is a very good mineral to give Gemini. Quartz has a very steady vibration rate and carrying a piece of it has a subtle effect, which can help keep the body balanced. One Gemini woman I know always wears earrings with cascades of tiny silver letters of the alphabet. It seems like a fitting image.

Gauze and other light fabrics that move in the breeze appeal to Gemini. Synthetic fabrics that are lightweight and durable are great because they are multipurpose. A reversible jacket would be a great Gemini gift.

Food, Herbs, Tastes, and Scents

In general these airy people are not strong on food or spices. They don't really pay that much attention to what they are eating if there is something more interesting going on. If you are raising a Gemini child, try to keep television and other stimuli to a minimum during meals. You'll find the child will eat more if he or she can concentrate on eating. Alphabet soup may be a favorite food. Geminis do like fruits and vegetables and food that can give them a quick burst of energy. A box of protein bars may be the easiest way for them to get nutrition. Your Gemini friend might appreciate a gift of a week of delivered meals. Herbs that are healthful for Gemini are dill and parsley. Herbs—such as echinacea, hops, and golden seal—that soothe the lungs and bronchi are very positive for Gemini.

Light floral scents—such as jasmine, lily of the valley, and gardenia—are perfect for Gemini. Eucalyptus oil in the winter months smells good and helps to keep the sinuses clear. Both male and female Gemini would enjoy being given an atomizer together with a variety of scents for the room. A book on aromatherapy would please curious Gemini.

Travel

Traveling for Gemini could be an "If it's Tuesday, it must be Belgium" experience. These restless people have no trouble being on the move and they thrive on different experiences. They are also fond of short trips and excursions. Planning a fabulous weekend jaunt to whisk Gemini away will win you big points. They also love practical gadgets that make being away from home simple. Palm pilots and ways to check e-mail even in the Sahara desert would be good gifts for mobile Gemini. Destinations that are traditionally associated with Gemini, such as London, are just close enough to make a quick trip appealing. A weekend in Gemini-ruled London going to the theater would be an excellent present. Other Gemini-ruled areas are Lombardy, Italy; Tripoli, Tunisia; and Cordova, Spain.

Sports

Gemini men and women enjoy sports that require bursts of energy rather than long endurance. They are usually sprinters rather than marathon runners. Their quick metabolism ensures that they could do both but they are apt to get too bored just pounding away until the twenty-sixth mile. Tennis, skiing, biking, hang gliding, or parachute jumping are all possible sports. A good yoga tape, chanting, or some other rhythmic breathing is a less exciting way for Gemini to relax and it can combat nervous exhaustion. You may find lots of ideas for gift-giving according to your Gemini's sport because he or she may have so many things lined up to do that they can't find time to get a racquet, or the required sneakers. Taking care of a small detail like that is a great gift for your speedy Gemini friends.

There are quite a few Gemini sports figures. Jim Thorpe is a perfect example of a multitalented Gemini. He competed in the pentathlon and the decathlon, as well as professional baseball and football. He was named "the athlete of the half century." Two noteworthy Gemini coaches are the late Vince Lombardi, of the Green Bay Packers, and Ara Parseghian, of Notre Dame. Both these people were known for their communication and motivational skills. Last, two major tennis stars, Don Budge, the first Grand Slam winner, and Steffi Graf, are Gemini. Tickets to sports events would always be welcome gifts.

Intellectual and Artistic Interests

All Geminis have a thirst for knowledge and revel in facts, trivia, and arcane knowledge, as well as philosophy and music. This is a sign that might welcome the *Encyclopaedia Britannica* on disc. Cancer loves the actual volumes but Gemini is most interested in the content. Consider also giving the collected works of Gemini Walt Whitman. Talking, rhyming, punning and turns of phrase are all very Gemini activities. Recorded books, language tapes, CDs of famous people speaking or reading would all appeal. Also, Gemini seems to have a fondness for fine writing paper and colorful stationery products. Purple file folders or green thumb tacks are the right touch of amusement and practicality for Gemini.

Many Geminis are multitalented. I encourage them to write a journal. If they can get some of the thoughts that whiz around their brain down on paper, it will allow room for other thoughts and may help them to organize themselves. Music is another artistic area for Gemini. Gemini people are often incredibly witty and funny. They can come up with puns and malapropisms and song lyrics that will keep their friends endlessly amused. A stand-up comedy course or open mike could be the beginning of a second career. Remember, Gemini's motto is "Do two."

Romance

Gemini and love is a kaleidoscopic whirl. The romance will never be boring but non-Gemini partners may be mystified at the sudden changes of plans and feelings. The best approach is to enjoy the changes and not expect a consistency that Gemini cannot deliver. Sharing activities is the best way to keep romance going with a Gemini. If you are apart, talking on the phone is a must. In fact, if you have an argument with your Gemini, you may be better off talking it out on the phone. It's easier for Gemini to listen when he or she is not distracted by emotional upsets. Gemini is interested in flirting and a committed partnership won't change this. After marriage there might be more looking and talking than action; if the non-Gemini has a jealous streak, some adjustments will have to be made.

Well-Known Gemini

Bob Dylan is a Gemini and his lyric "the answers, my friend, is blowing in the wind" epitomizes the Gemini's free and easy approach to life and problem solving. If your Gemini is in need of a lift, give the sound track to the film *Casino Royale*; the brass intro is as good as an antidepressant. Cole Porter, composer of classics such as "Begin the Beguine," was a Gemini. Without even knowing the tune, you can hear the music in his lyrics. And of course, one of the most famous Gemini musicians is Sir Paul McCartney. John Lennon was a Libra and these two air-sign artists enjoyed a rare artistic collaboration. The entire rap genre is the kind of oral poetry that Gemini would invent. I wonder if there is a preponderance of Gemini among rappers? Two well-known Gemini rappers are Mark Wahlberg and the late Tupac Shakur.

In classical music, the composers Robert Schumann, Richard Strauss, and Richard Wagner were all Gemini. Wagner was probably one of the most interesting artists of the nineteenth century. In addition to his operas, he wrote volumes of essays on aesthetics. He wanted to create a total music drama where the story of the opera, the poetry, the scenery, and the music all served to transport the audience to another realm. His major work, *The Ring Cycle*, is monumental. It takes hours to listen to all four operas but it is quite an unforgettable experience. If you and your Gemini friend decide to plan a Wagner weekend, follow the operas with the scores. The stories are intricate.

In literature there is a wide variety of Gemini authors. Two of the most popular were Ian Fleming, the creator of the James Bond books, and Arthur Conan Doyle, creator of Sherlock Holmes. The plots in these books are fascinating puzzles and would give endless delight to your Gemini. Another author who personifies the youthful wit that Geminis retain throughout their lives is Maurice Sendak. His children's books entertain people of all ages. Other contemporary authors are Joyce Carol Oates, the playwright Athol Fugard, and Salman Rushdie.

Before looking at showbiz celebrities, it is interesting to note that two prominent scientists were Gemini and female. Barbara McClintock, who was a geneticist, won the Nobel Prize at age 81. Rachel Carson, who wrote *Silent Spring*, was a marine biologist and one of the first voices in the ecology movement. Another great contributor to marine biology and ecology was Jacques Cousteau. All three of these scientists communicated to a wide audience and so publicized their fields to give the message that all life is connected.

Witty word play, spoofs, and jokes are a Gemini forte. Actor and comedian Paul Lynde was a Gemini; after many years as a performer he made his living being the resident wit and "center square" on *Hollywood Squares*. Another major comedian is Bob Hope. A collection of his *Road* pictures with Bing Crosby has enough variety and silly jokes to keep even restless Gemini amused. If you get bored with these films consider all of John Wayne's films. The Duke was a Gemini. The brilliant mimic, writer, actor, and comedian Mike Myers is a Gemini. Another star with great chameleon abilities is Johnny Depp.

Perhaps the best-known female Gemini was Marilyn Monroe. Although she was recognized primarily for her beauty and complicated love relationships, she had a sharp mind. The amount of information and communication her memory provokes even today is a testament to the thought-provoking complexities of her Gemini personality. Another Gemini actress is Joan Rivers whose "Can we talk?" is a phrase any Gemini can relate to. Other well-known Gemini are Brooke Shields, Elizabeth Hurley, Isabella Rossellini, Nicole Kidman, and Courteney Cox.

Gemini: Response to Celebrations and Occasions

BIRTHDAY

A surprise party or gathering of friends may be the best way to celebrate a Gemini's birthday. The sign's motto is "Do Two." First have a large party; then have a quieter gathering for close friends and family. Since Gemini's birthday usually falls when the weather is fine, a picnic or outdoor meal where there are sports, swans, and canoes—i.e., lots of activity—is a perfect choice to keep this changeable nature interested and feeling celebrated.

CHRISTMAS / HANUKAH

The December holidays fall in the very opposite time of the year to Gemini's natal turf. These people do not usually like the bulkiness of winter clothes or combating the weather. The ski slopes would be the best place for Gemini to enjoy winter. Indoor activities for Gemini include writing, drawing, talking on the phone, and games of all sorts. If the game is intricate, it will keep Gemini absorbed for hours and is good for long winter days and nights.

ENGAGEMENT / MARRIAGE

An engagement announces a pairing that, for Gemini, means someone to talk to forever. Plan on a bachelor party for the groom and bridal showers for the bride. Presents should speak to the couple's interests rather than building their home. Butterfly motifs are the perfect symbol for two Gemini hitching up. A Gemini views marriage as the opportunity to maximize fun and minimize restrictions and traditions.

Think light and airy and do not weigh these people down with the "supposed to" silver and crystal. Both Gemini brides and grooms will, however, enjoy good quality monogrammed stationery.

New Baby

To Gemini parents a baby is an exercise in brisk management. These parents will be very creative in how they teach and stimulate their kids. Gifts that will promote education, learning, intellectual stimulation, are the important values for Gemini parents. If the baby is a Gemini, a mobile with lots of colors is a good gift. Also expect the baby to begin speaking early. If you would like a child to be bilingual, the Gemini is a natural. Make sure the baby gets enough time outside; fresh air is important for Gemini.

New Home

The house will probably have tons of windows and you might want to give a window washing service as a gift! Wind chimes and prisms that reflect the light are a good idea. Bookshelves are usually welcome, as is furniture that can be used in two or more ways, like a sofa bed. Change in the home is Gemini's lifeblood. Many Gemini are rarely in their homes. The best housewarming gift may be airplane tickets.

Anniversary

Take him or her out. Gemini want to feel the thrill of romance on their anniversary rather than the comforts of home. An adventure, trip, or special activity, such as a lecture series or concert, is the perfect Gemini activity. Writing down some noteworthy event of the past year or creating a notebook of good times could be a special Gemini present. Remember: Do two. If you get a sentimental present, accompany it with a humorous, silly present. Gemini need both sides of their personality tickled.

VALENTINE'S DAY

Wispy flowers or that interesting book he or she has wanted is the ticket here. A Gemini's mind moves too quickly for it to be entertained by romance for long. If your Gemini has a sweet tooth, consider white chocolate. Remember that Cupid was the messenger of love and Gemini loves messages. An image of Cupid bringing 100 Valentines could be a prized gift. A red telephone to be used only for hot conversations or making up after a lovers' quarrel would be a catchy gift.

MOTHER'S DAY

Motherhood for a Gemini is a fascinating inquiry into baby behavior and communication. She considers being a mother her job so she cherishes time off. She doesn't gush. She teaches and communicates to her children. On her day she wants a baby-sitter and a chance to do something for herself that would bolster her mental development and interests.

FATHER'S DAY

Gemini fathers are excellent communicators and like to know that their message is getting through. He would particularly enjoy a father/daughter or father/son interesting special event for Father's Day. Gemini fathers are great playmates and this is the day that the dads should be able to choose the toys. He might love a trip in a hot air balloon.

GRADUATION

Finishing school at whatever level is the entrance into a wider world in which to communicate. Many Gemini work as salespeople no matter what they have studied in school. Current computer technology or software and Internet savvy may be the best focus for Gemini graduation gifts. A fountain pen or pen set would also be welcome.

THANK-YOU PRESENT

Gemini delights in witty cards or cards with intricate visual designs. The traditional gifts of flowers or sweets will not be as meaningful as a book or something that cleverly states your message. A singing telegram, or a comedy-gram, would be the best gift. A bunch of balloons with thanks in different languages could be the highlight of a Gemini's day.

ANYTIME PRESENT

Choose a subscription to a magazine or newspaper that your Gemini is not expecting. Then when he/she gets it in the mail the pleasure will be doubled. Gemini loves to be surprised. Flowers, silver jewelry or a surprise outing are also possibilities.

Gemini Gift Suggestions

GEMINI MAN

Thrifty Saturn

Outdoor/indoor thermometer
How-to books
Reversible jacket
A good dictionary
Air gun
Tickets to a concert/lecture
John Wayne videos
Chess set
Book of quotable quotes
Mechanical pencil

Luxurious Venus

Dual time zone watch
Colored cell phone
Aquamarine cuff links
Blond wood desk
Striped shirts
Sales tips books
Trip to Versailles, France
First edition book by a favorite author
A lightweight briefcase
A butterfly collection

Bountiful Jupiter

Private jet
House on stilts
Personal traffic light

Portable tape recorder
Beryl paperweight
Penthouse
A vintage Cadillac
Monogrammed underwear
Lifetime tickets to the Knicks
Sailboat
A hot-air balloon

GEMINI WOMAN

Thrifty Saturn

Light blue scarf
Airmail stationery
Private phone booth
Monogrammed stationery
Magazine subscriptions
Gardenia soap
Silver bangle bracelets
Pocket organizer
Rattan baskets
Magazine rack
Bamboo screen

Luxurious Venus

Sheer organza
Trip to the Twin Cities
(Minneapolis and St. Paul)
Dinner on top of a skyscraper
Subscription concert tickets
Reversible blue/silver jacket
Bicycle built for two
Matched luggage

Double terminated quartz crystal
Feng shui compass
A ceiling fan
Pet parrot
Printmaker program

Bountiful Jupiter

Butterfly rug
Marionette theater
Grove of palm trees
Two homes
Wicker sleigh bed
Twin porches
Car with driver
Colorful computers
Ornate birdcages
Bright blue Mazda
Tennis court
Wind surfing boat

GEMINI BOYS AND TEENS

Popsicle stick mobile
Colored pencils
Reams of drawing paper
Guinea pig
Flashcards
Talking action figure
Balloons
Cotton candy
Felt-tipped pens
Remote control airplane or sailboat
Mechanical toys

Egyptian hieroglyphics
A travel atlas
A parrot
Drum brushes
Songs by Bob Dylan
Team pennants
Magazine subscription
Tennis balls
A whistle
A pachinko machine
Pocket translator
Morse code machine
A monkey
A typewriter

GEMINI GIRLS AND TEENS

Musical note stencil
Ornate fingernails
Colored pencils
Silver ID bracelet
Paper chains
Walkie-talkie
Talking doll
Travel posters
Stuffed toy penguin
Beryl power bracelet
Pop-up books
Fashion gloves
Silver secret box
Etch-A-sketch
A diary
Cheerleading pom-poms

Feather earrings
Canopy bed
Gauzy clothing
Language lessons
A pen pal
A lighted globe
Spiral notebooks
Pencil cases
Twin puppies
Batons
Collection of fans

Cancer
June 21–July 22

CANCER
A Cardinal Yin Sign

SYMBOL:	The Crab
RULING PLANET:	Moon
ELEMENT:	Water
BODY PART:	Breasts, chest, stomach
FAVORED POSSESSIONS:	Childhood mementos, antiques, home gadgets
COMMUNICATION STYLE:	Feeling and sentimental
HOME STYLE:	Traditional and soothing
COLORS AND METAL:	Gray, dark blue, silver
FOOD, PLANTS, FLOWERS:	Milk, shellfish, maple trees, verbena, water lily
PARTNERSHIP STYLE:	Nurturing and protective
RULING PASSION:	To live in tune with moods and feeling
PHILOSOPHY:	Family and feelings first
GEMSTONES:	Pearls, moonstones
WISHES OR GOALS:	To protect personal feelings
UNCONSCIOUS DESIRE:	To control the personal environment
FOR GIFT-GIVING, KEEP IN MIND:	Cancer likes personal gifts of sentiment and meaning.

Character Traits and Symbols

Cancer is the second cardinal sign of the zodiac. The beginning of Cancer is the summer solstice. The famous Cancerian moodiness is sometimes thought to be a sign of a shy, retiring nature; however, cardinal signs are leadership signs and Cancer is no exception. These people lead indirectly. It can drive the more direct fire signs wild as they are convinced that this moody Cancer will never accomplish what he or she sets out to do, but time will prove that the Cancerian generally achieves his or her goal. Cancer's hand-wringing, tears, and back and forth feelings can try the patience of everyone around them, but they'll get where they are going. Crabs, the symbol for Cancer, are half land and half water creatures. The moods of this sign are necessary to their forward progress. They make a move on dry land, a metaphor for worldly life, and then dip back into the water, which represents their feelings and spiritual life, to renew themselves and to tap into their intuition in order to see if it is safe to proceed.

The moonchild loves gifts of sentiment that show your feelings and speak to Cancer's feelings. Don't be surprised if Cancer's response to a gift is initially polite but not enthusiastic. If you have chosen well, their true feelings or enjoyment sets in after he or she feels familiar with this new object or experience.

Water is Cancer's element and the moon its ruling planet. Cancer is a receptive sign and absorbs atmospheres and experiences with their entire being. Cancer loves the seashore but is not keen on bright sunlight. I have often thought a portable screened-in porch or a large tent would be the perfect way for Cancer to experience the beach. He or she could take a walk by the water and then retreat into the shade.

One of the strongest traits of Cancer is the urge to hold on to the past. Past memories can be as vivid as present realities and Cancer may spend a lot of time rehashing past experiences. There is an intrinsic pleasure for Cancer when they revisit the known and familiar. Diaries, scrapbooks, old recordings and sheet music all evoke the past. When I say "the past," I mean both a person's personal past and the historical past. Most Cancers enjoy antiques and if the object is something that they grew up with, you have a doubleheader.

Photography and all recording equipment suit Cancer because they love to capture moments to mull over at a later time. The undisputed genius of remembrance and capturing moments of the past was Cancerian Marcel Proust. If your Cancerian likes to read, Proust's *Remembrance of Things Past* might be a pleasing gift. Photographic equipment that allows your Cancerian to make his/her own supply of past images is also a perfect spur to creativity; a six-month supply of disposable cameras might be as appreciated as a fancy video recorder.

Another interest of Cancerians is family heirlooms and traditions. Genealogical trees, family memorabilia, ancestors' biographies, family crests, family skeletons or mysteries, military medals, or other treasures that pertain to the family are very good places to look for gifts. One Cancerian family I know held a family reunion and one of the hosts had found a set of voice recordings by family members who had passed away. She bought an old phonograph, and by playing the records, she created the illusion that the whole family was present.

In the business world, Cancer often uses his hard shell and tenacity to hold tight to money and status. Although Cancerians will wax sentimental about staying home, they usually like to be in the flow of business and important positions. Cancer loves money and can attract resources. The sign needs security and money soothes that drive. Often their financial acumen is not the result of thought or strategy but comes from following their instincts and feelings. One Cancerian client accumulated a small fortune and claimed that he only did business with people he felt comfortable with, no matter how good "the deal" looked on paper. Lucky pennies, a money clip with the person's business logo, the first dollar ever earned framed—these are all appropriate gifts for Cancer. Also, I have noticed that many Cancerian men have an antique ship in a bottle in their offices.

Perhaps the image of the wide seas contained in a safe bottle gets at the heart of the dichotomy of Cancer's love of motion and security. An excellent suggestion for all Cancerians is a lunar calendar that shows the phases of the moon. If your Cancerian keeps track of the lunar cycle, he or she will feel more initiative and energy between the new and full moon. While the moon is waning it's time to relax and prepare for the next burst of energy.

The home is Cancer's favorite sphere and should be cozy and warm. In terms of style, Cancer likes modern updates of classical styles. The basic need of all Cancerians is to move into the future with memories and experiences from the past that serve them rather than bog them down. If Cancerians can surround themselves with furniture, household items, radios, or designs that remind them of pleasant memories from their past, they will feel encouraged to move into the future. Anything that has bad associations should be thrown out or it could remind Cancer of the time he or she didn't feel good at Aunt Emma's and then a mood will descend. A breezier sign like Aquarius, who lives in the future, may be dumbfounded to observe how Cancer can feel physically uncomfortable from objects that remind them of unpleasant memories.

The bathroom is a favorite room. Cancer does not like to fool around with mediocre plumbing. The shower or bathwater should be hot and plentiful. Gifts of bath soaps, oils, bubble bath, or a few rubber ducks will always be appreciated. Frog bathtub toys are also a good idea for all ages. No Cancerian is too old to play with toys in the tub. If you can find a big old-fashioned tub, it would combine Cancer's historical interests with watery comfort. Needless to say, a Jacuzzi is a great luxury gift.

Cancer, like all water signs, is sensitive to noise. If you live in a city, consider giving a set of soothing tapes or even a white-noise machine to muffle traffic, sirens, etc. The sign of Cancer rules New York City; I imagine for all the harmony that a Cancerian may enjoy there the noise pollution is a big strain on the nervous system. Investigate what kind of music your Cancerian enjoys; giving him or her a Walkman is the best way of creating a bubble of sound insulation. A year's supply of earplugs may solve a good deal of Cancer's crankiness with the outside world.

In nature, Cancerians prefer shade. Forests with a small stream or creek may be preferable to the harsh sunlight and heat of the beach. If you do live near the sea, you may notice that your Cancerian friends or family want to connect with the ocean as winter ebbs. With the first signs of spring, Cancerians will often propose a trip to the ocean. In your home yard a lily pond with a few resident frogs would be a perfect place for Cancer to calm his thoughts and dream. Frogs are Cancerian animals; their skin is extremely sensitive and they live on both water and land. One Cancerian woman I know decorated her entire house with frog knickknacks and designs. I thought having Kermit the frog pillows on her sofa was a little extreme, but if it made her happy, I didn't think I should comment.

The lunar laugh is an unmistakable part of the Cancerian personality. Once you have heard this sound, which can sound like a whooping or a manic cackle, you will enjoy giving gifts that make your Cancerian laugh. Humor videos, old radio comedy tapes and cartoons stimulate Cancer's imagination. All Cancerians have a great deal of silliness to their nature and bringing out the childlike joy in humor is the best antidote to Cancer's moody blues.

Colors and Flowers

The basic color palette is gentle and Cancers are fond of black and white. Midnight blue, gray, olive green, sage, pale green and khaki are also all good choices. Usually Cancer likes to wear colors that blend in with other people. Shimmering fabrics especially in gray or silver remind Cancer of the moon. Cancer is partial to night-blooming flowers. Irises, water violets, and white saxifrage are also flowers that appeal to Cancer. Having a greenhouse where they can putter and nurture plants would be a luxury gift for Cancerians. Trees rich in sap such as maple, olive, and palm are all Cancer-ruled. There are beautiful carved bowls and salad spoons made from olive wood. They would be a wonderful gift.

Metals, Gems, and Materials

The metal associated with Cancer is silver. You might notice that Cancerians frequently wear many silver rings or have a silver necklace with one pearl drop. Aluminum is also a Cancerian metal. It may not be the best choice for jewelry but there are many household items made from brushed aluminum that are very attractive.

Quartz crystal is a good mineral for Cancer; the steady vibration of clear quartz can regulate Cancer's changeable and moody nature. White pearls, both freshwater and cultured, are also Cancerian gems. One Cancerian lady had one piece of jewelry: a string of large matched white pearls. When her friend protested that they were too valuable to wear on the street, the Cancerian said, "No one believes they are real, and besides, they make me feel good." The translucent stone moonstone is fittingly a Cancerian stone. Also, milky opals and milk-white stones belong to moonchildren.

A creative gift for a Cancerian child would be a comforter or bedspread made from old clothes that the child has outgrown. The memories that the material recalls and the soft feel of worn fabric makes a comfortable security blanket for children (or adults). Cancerians also hate waste. They will not throw leftovers out, and if clothes and household goods can be recycled or fixed, they are thrilled. All material that shimmers and feels smooth appeals to Cancer.

Food, Herbs, Tastes, and Scents

Both Cancerian men and women have strong nurturing instincts and show their love with food. The stomach is sensitive and Cancerian children who complain of stomachaches usually are nervous about something. Discordant mealtimes will give any Cancerian nervous indigestion. Many moonchildren are very good cooks and prefer to cook at home rather than eat out. They enjoy sweet and salty tastes and may appreciate specialty food items from the sea.

Sardines, smoked oysters, mussels, anchovies, and kippers all please Cancer's palate. As a chef, the Cancer man or woman likes labor-saving gadgets. I know one man who outfitted his small kitchen with a deli-size meat slicer, a French fry cooker, a restaurant-quality pancake griddle, a waffle iron, and a special mixer for milk shakes. He wanted to be sure he could fix whatever he or his guests desired. Gadgets that make life easier are great gifts for your Cancer. If he likes coffee, then a streamlined state of the art coffeemaker is perfect. Buy one for traveling, as Cancer likes to have his comforts with him in unfamiliar circumstances.

Herbs and spices for Cancer tend to be mild. Rosemary, oregano, sage, and all herbs that promote digestion are beneficial. An old-fashioned wooden spice rack would be an excellent gift.

Since Cancerian skin is usually very sensitive, they appreciate gifts of bath lotion, skin creams, aftershave or cologne. The preferred scents are mild florals or mint for both men and women. A good sunblock is a must.

Travel

Travel can be dicey for the Crab as he requires a sense of home even on the road. Too many nights in different hotels are very wearing on the system. Nevertheless, Cancer is attracted to travel, especially to places where there is a point of historical interest. All Cancerians have a vivid sense of history and can imagine themselves living in different historical times. One Cancer I knew had a terrible sense of

direction until he got to Venice. He pretended he was
an Italian Renaissance artist and he knew exactly
how to get everywhere he wanted to go. It was almost as if he were remembering a past life. Cruise
travel or a trip on a barge down a river would be a
great gift for Cancer. Many of the world's most beautiful cities such as Amsterdam, Venice, and Istanbul
are Cancerian cities. The United States, "born" on
the Fourth of July, is a Cancerian nation.

Sports

Cancerians are generally not keen on exercise.
When they are in the mood, they may enjoy it, but
if they are feeling out of sorts, the physical exertion
agitates their system. They may love to play in the
water but I have seen that frequently Cancerians are
slightly fearful of water and do not like to swim.
They can enjoy solitary exercise such as cross-country
skiing or running. Walking and hiking may be the
best way to stretch the body. A gentle aerobic workout tape could be the best gift. Cancer likes music
and usually has an innate sense of rhythm.

There are a number of sports celebrities who are
Cancerian. Contrary to the sign's element of water, I
found very few swimmers or divers here, but there
are many gold medal figure skaters: Kristi Yama-
guchi, Dick Button, and Tenley Albright are some of
the most prominent. The greatest all-around female
athlete of all time, Mildred "Babe" Zaharias, was a
Cancer. She won two Olympic gold medals in track
and was a professional golf champion. Two great
prizefighters—Mike Tyson and Jack Dempsey—are

also Cancers. This might be encouraging news for Cancerians who prefer watching the fights to exercising.

Intellectual and Artistic Interests

All historical time periods interest Cancer. They are frequently very interested in military histories because Cancer is a very patriotic sign. World War II memorabilia, videos, and photographic essays are usually interesting to Cancerian men whether they were in the service or not.

Cancer is also a very artistic sign. Music attracts Cancerians as do the performing and the visual arts. If a Cancerian can overcome stage fright he is usually a versatile performer, because he or she can convey so many different feelings. If Cancer children are given music or art lessons when they are young, it will stay with them for life. Drawing is a very focusing activity for adult Cancerians. A gift of different charcoals and drawing pencils would encourage their artistic talents. Cancerians are also excellent photographers. Get them started with the hobby and it will interest them for life.

Romance

Cancerians in love will not be deterred in their pursuit for "the one." These people do not give their hearts easily, but when they do it is for keeps. Sentiment rules the Cancerian and a romance with these sensitive souls means lots of kissing and making up as each clarifies how they didn't mean to hurt the other's feelings. The urge to create a home and a family unit is strong. Both Cancerian men and women will want to mother their sweeties. They are attentive, rarely forget birthdays and anniversaries, and are interested in continuity. The most important gift could be time alone so the Cancerian can stabilize his or her feelings. Then you and your Cancerian love can head for the bathtub. It will soothe both of you and make even thorny problems melt away. A weekend getaway where there is an outdoor Jacuzzi could probably solve the problems of the world!

Well-Known Cancerians

If you look at a list of notable artists, a good number of painters are Cancers. A major genius was Rembrandt. His portraits and self-portraits are masterpieces. A trip to the museum or a book of Rembrandt's work would be a treasured gift. Other wonderful Cancerian painters include Reubens, Marc Chagall, Frida Kahlo, Degas, and Andrew Wyeth. Wyeth's painting *Christina's World* conveys the feeling of longing for home, which is a Cancerian trait. It is also interesting to note that Whistler was a Cancerian and his most famous painting is popularly known as *Whistler's Mother*. Cancerians either have a close relationship with their mothers or are estranged.

A number of very funny performers are Cancers. Mel Brooks, Robin Williams, Bill Cosby, and Phyllis Diller are all moonchildren. There is something outrageous about the humor of all these people. Mel Brooks' movie and Broadway musical, *The Producers*, takes a simple idea and creates lunacy and satire. I think only a Cancerian could have come up with an idea like "Springtime for Hitler." If this reference eludes you, ask your Cancerian friends or rent the movie. The very versatile actor James Cagney was a Cancer. If you look at his film *White Heat*, it is a portrait of a mama complex gone bad. Two-time Academy Award winner Tom Hanks is a Cancerian. Stephen Lang, a versatile stage, television (*The Fugitive*), and film actor has a wonderful combination of sweetness and toughness that characterizes the Cancerian personality. The up-and-coming actor Billy Crudup is also Cancer. An interesting gift for Cancerians would be the classic video of *The Hunchback of Notre Dame*. Charles Laughton's performance as the hunchback is heartrending.

Many high-powered actresses belong to Cancer. Meryl Streep was born just after the summer solstice. People joke that many of her movies are five-handkerchief weepies, but like many Cancerians she has so many emotions that tears are frequent; she is an extraordinary performer. Other Cancer actresses are Diana Rigg, Barbara Stanwyck, Angelica Huston, and Didi Conn. Give your Cancerian a video of the film *Grease* and look at Didi Conn's number, "Beauty School Dropout." It is hilarious.

One of the most well-known Cancerian musicians is Louis Armstrong. Louis Armstrong, born on the Fourth of July, brought jazz into the mainstream. He had a warmth and sensitivity that typifies moonchildren. The songwriting team of Rodgers and Hammerstein, who created the musicals *South Pacific, The Sound of Music, Carousel,* and *Flower Drum Song,* was a Cancerian duo. As you might expect, they both worked at home. Classical music lovers would enjoy works by Gustav Mahler, and opera buffs will love recordings by two of the greatest singers, Cancerians Nicolai Gedda and Hermann Prey.

In the field of humanitarian accomplishments, Nelson Mandela and the Dalai Lama are both Cancers. Mandela's collected works of his struggle in prison and his work for the dignity of his people are inspirational. The Dalai Lama also has written numerous books that would be perfect gifts for any Cancerian. My favorite is *The Art of Happiness*.

Cancer: Response to Celebrations and Occasions

BIRTHDAY

Stay home and have a family gathering. Cancers have a sentimental attachment to holidays and are very sensitive to the feelings that surround a celebration. No getting older or larger jokes, please! Cancer lacks the tough hide to repel comments made even in jest. Apple pie, chocolate cake with white frosting, or anything that means home and comfort should be part of the party. Picture-taking is also a good idea to commemorate the occasion.

CHRISTMAS / HANUKAH

The December holidays are astrologically at the opposite time of the year from Cancer. The holiday is usually a low energy point for the moonchild, who may be a bit blue at this time of the year. While festivities can be the cure for winter depression, they can also prick Cancer's sensitivity. This is a time of great feeling and clinging close to the known. Don't expect to go far from home at Christmas and choose presents, carefully, for your ultrasensitive Cancer. Bursting into tears on Christmas is not unheard of.

ENGAGEMENT / MARRIAGE

Cancerian people may be among the few that actually court or are courted. When the engagement is announced they want their time for the families to gather together and throw a shower. Meet at one person's home at the full moon and give gifts that are traditional and long lasting. Cancers relate strongly to the idea of building a home together and will want to create a cozy nest. A collage of baby pictures of either the bride or groom is a great idea. At the wedding, make sure that the photographer is unobtrusive. Cancer does not want to be jostled or self-conscious in sensitive moments. Cancer brides and grooms will adhere to tradition in some way. The brides will have something old, something borrowed, or something blue, and the groom will respect the custom of not seeing the bride in her wedding dress before the ceremony.

New Baby

Welcoming a new baby into the family makes Cancer parents swell with feeling because there will be family continuity and lots of opportunities to watch cartoons together. New parents will enjoy privacy for the first few days and then will enjoy introducing the baby to the clan. If the baby is born under the sign of Cancer, definitely give the parents a lunar calendar so they can chart the kid's moods. Also buy the newest book on how to get kids to sleep through the night. Cancerian babies seem to enjoy late nights and parents might not appreciate their nocturnal hours.

New Home

Need I say anything? A home is the place to be for Cancer and any gifts that increase ease or comfort there will be welcome and appreciated. A good stereo or media center is a great idea. Cancer usually likes music and old recordings. Colored drinking glasses would also be a good choice.

ANNIVERSARY

Just don't forget it! Both Cancer husbands and wives would seriously consider separation if such a thing occurred. I would recommend a familiar restaurant that is special. Cancerians like to go out as long as there are no crowds, no lines to wait in, and a good quiet corner booth to sit in and dream of all the good times that have been and are to come.

VALENTINE'S DAY

Some Cancerian men may hate this holiday because it obliges them to be romantic when they believe they are romantic most of the time. Both Cancerian men and women will enjoy a special card that reminds them of past romantic times, or a little love token, such as a box of matches from a restaurant that is special to them. One Cancerian man I know gave his love a frog in a terrarium because they really enjoyed walking in the country and looking for frogs.

MOTHER'S DAY

This holiday was designed for Cancerian women. Their sign symbolizes the great mother, nurturing, and all that is protective in mother love. Let the kids cook dinner for Mom; even if it is a catastrophe of a tuna casserole, she will love it and sniffle because her babies have grown so big and clever. Older children may enjoy offering a gourmet dinner served in the dining room. A more casual Cancerian mom might just love takeout!

FATHER'S DAY

The Cancerian father is usually a contented parent with a tendency toward benevolent dictatorship.

Granting permission to sleep late and then serving a pancake breakfast would be a good way to celebrate Dad's day. He won't mind having the whole clan over for a barbecue as long as it is clear that he can stop cooking or hosting if his mood changes.

THANK-YOU PRESENT

If you are invited to a Cancer's home, the experience will warrant a present. These folks love to extend themselves and their homes to others as long as they have their own corner where they can retreat. Consider giving a small piece of crystal or a night-blooming plant. For other occasions consider a book or a batch of homemade cookies. Cancer would also be happy with a warm hug.

ANYTIME PRESENT

Cancer won't mind at all if you give him or her a domestic present. A pair of socks that reminded you of him or her is as welcome as an expensive piece of jewelry. Doing an errand for the sometimes lazy Cancer is also a wonderful gift. Give the present with affection and it won't matter what it is.

Cancer Gift Suggestions

CANCER MAN

Thrifty Saturn

Goldfish bowl
Home gadgets
Photography equipment
Fisherman's cap
High power shower head
Gray sweater
Money clip
Ice cream maker
Seafood cookbook
Gourmet smoked fish
Beer steins
Famous Monsters magazines
Homemade meal

Luxurious Venus

Investment information
Trip on a barge
Antique bottles
Woodworking kit
Leather bound books
A greenhouse
A juicer
Mother of pearl cuff links
Silver key chain
Home brewery
Trip to Holland
Historical radio show tapes

Beach club membership

Bountiful Jupiter

A yacht
Home on the water
A lighthouse
A bed and breakfast
Cork-lined room
A large aquarium
A pocket watch
Trip to see Galapagos tortoises
Cruise around the world
Grove of willow trees
Personal bank
Vintage Triumph 4

CANCER WOMAN

Thrifty Saturn

Wooden cupboards
Daisies
Apple pie recipes
A shrimp dinner
White poppies
Antique milk bottles
Aluminum glasses
Pearls on a silver chain
Linen dish towels
Soup pot
Blue Depression glass
Moon-shaped candles

Luxurious Venus

White percale sheets
Mambo music
Silver tea service
Jasmine perfume
A fountain
Moonstone ring
Chandelier
Tortoiseshell combs
Life supply of crab cakes
Night-blooming cereus
Pearls

Bountiful Jupiter

Indoor/outdoor pool
String of Tahitian pearls
An ancient sculpture
Personal dairy
Bathhouse
Watered silk clothes
An island
Restaurant stove
A beautiful home
Personal Jacuzzi
A trip to Istanbul

CANCER BOYS AND TEENS

Moon stickers
Frog pajamas
Seashells
Colored chalk
Toy sailboat

Designer sunglasses
Blue-green sweater
A canoe
Cellar playroom
Lily pond
A mushroom garden
A camera/video recorder
Trip to New York City
Surfboard
Black shirts
Lunar phase calendar
A cookbook
Vintage comic books
Cartoon videos
An owl
Military history books
Boogie-woogie records
Water pistols
A jet ski
A water slide

CANCER GIRLS AND TEENS

Crescent-shaped jewelry
Baker's cap
Silver sparkly paper
Shell bracelet
Water pistols
Moon night light
A turtle
A sailor's hat
Illustrated fairy tales
Water ballet lessons

Add-a-pearl necklace
A lily pond
A silver locket
Wintergreen scent
Tickets to a cabaret
Savings account
Moonstone earrings
Cucumber astringent/soap
Rose de mai aroma
Silver thumb ring
Bubble bath
A hamster
A crab net
Bead stringing kit

Leo
July 23–August 22

LEO
A Fixed Yang Sign

SYMBOL:	The Lion
RULING PLANET:	The Sun
ELEMENT:	Fire
BODY PART:	Heart, spine, and back
FAVORED POSSESSIONS:	A mirror, a star, a throne-like chair
COMMUNICATION STYLE:	Dramatic and commanding
HOME STYLE:	Showy and large
COLORS AND METAL:	Bright yellow, orange, gold
FOOD, PLANTS, FLOWERS:	Walnuts, bay leaves, rice, sunflowers
PARTNERSHIP STYLE:	Generous and dominant
RULING PASSION:	To live in the spotlight
PHILOSOPHY:	Emphasize generosity and forgiveness
GEMSTONES:	Ruby, cat's eye, amber
WISHES OR GOALS:	To reign over an entertaining world
FOR GIFT-GIVING, KEEP IN MIND:	Leo likes noticeable gifts with lots of flair

$\mathcal{S}$

Character Traits and Symbols

Leo is the second fixed sign of the zodiac. Deep summer, when the living is easy, is Leo's time. This sign is pleasure-loving and very expansive. There is no other sign that is as generous. Leos love gifts that announce their importance and regal nature: Think luxurious and prominent. It's not that Leos are materialistic—they just want to be acknowledged for their gift of leadership and nobility. After all, Leo is the king or queen of the jungle, and with the sun as their ruling planet, Leo wants to shine brightly. Many Leos, both children and adults, love to put on crowns at a birthday party. A gold tiara would be a perfect gift to give to a special Leo. Leos have a lot of charisma and are aware that they make a good impression on people. Inside, however, they often feel insecure and search for approval. This part of their personality is hidden, as their pride inhibits showing insecurity. If you find gifts that speak to a

Leo's hunger for attention, you will have a magnanimous friend for life.

Leo's symbol is, of course, the Lion. The astrological symbol is thought to be the lion's curled tail or an emblem representing the phallus, as used in ancient Dionysian mysteries. Leo is the most vital sign of the zodiac and has tremendous energy. The myth of Phaëthon driving his father's (the Sun's) chariot is one to consider for Leo. The myth tells that Phaëthon, who was a mortal on his mother's side, came to the palace of the Sun to find out if the Sun was indeed his father. The Sun was touched by the boy's sincerity and told him that he was his father. To prove his love he offered the boy anything he wanted. Phaëthon asked to drive his father's chariot. The Sun recognized that he had to fulfill his promise, but realizing that doing so would probably destroy the boy, he tried to dissuade him. Phaëthon would not listen and when he lost control of the reins the Sun's chariot dipped so near the earth that it threatened to burn the earth. Zeus intervened and threw a thunderbolt at the chariot and struck Phaëthon dead. The story's meaning is clear. If the immature ego drives the personality (symbolized by the Sun's chariot) there can be pain and meltdown. If the mature self is at the reins, then Leo can cooperate and share his enthusiasm and fire with others. The course of any Leo's life will be determined by the extent to which they can shine with other people.

Fire is Leo's element and like all fire signs they have the ability to inspire. The fire signs have good hunches and should follow them. Leo is also the sign of the father. In traditional societies the father as head of the household meditated and prayed for guidance for his entire family. He was the leader and bore the responsibility for the successes of the family. Both Leo men and women feel this responsibility and want to be appreciated and respected for their efforts.

The heart and the spine are the areas of the body ruled by Leo. The spine is the cord of energy that keeps the entire body energized. Leo needs to keep the spine flexible so his vitality can spread throughout the body. Leo is a fixed sign, and all the powerhouse fixed signs (Taurus, Scorpio, and Aquarius) benefit from yoga or gentle stretching rather than activities that pound the body. Yoga tapes, music to exercise with, or a sun lamp to keep the body warm are great ideas for Leo. One yoga teacher held a class for people over sixty, and there was one woman who was in great shape and could hold the most difficult poses for quite some time. The teacher asked her how old she was and was astounded to learn she was seventy-seven. When the teacher asked how she stayed in such good shape, the lady replied, "I exercise, eat a little of everything . . . and I'm a Leo." The yoga teacher loved this because she was Leo also.

You may particularly notice Leo's mane of hair; it is usually thick and wavy and a great pleasure to him or her. Hair-grooming products and special gels in citrus or spicy smells please Leo. If your Leo does not like the smell of a product, he or she will not use it. Women may enjoy a large collection of barrettes and scrunchies with a variety of hairstyles. For Leo men, a haircut can be a traumatic experience. I have not figured out whether this is the Samson dilemma or just that Leo feels so possessive about his hair that seeing less of it jars them. A bad haircut depresses both Leo men and women and they will be ruthlessly critical of any hairdresser who doesn't make the grade.

Leo shines in all work that requires presentations or interaction with people. Special event coordinators, marketing executives, and actors and actresses are frequently found in this sign. Teachers born under Leo are always interesting and effective. They are not always patient. No matter what type of work your Leo does, consider buying him a star for his dressing room or bathroom door. A spotlight wouldn't be a bad idea either. There are some Leos who do not like the center of attention and are subject to stage fright. A great gift for these quiet cats would be acting lessons or classes in public speaking. All Leos do not have to be front and center but most enjoy being publicly saluted. Encouragement is essential for them.

Gambling establishments and games of chance belong to Leo. Card games of all kinds appeal to them. The sign loves the thrill of taking a chance but usually can moderate its passion for winning if the dice or cards turn against them. Leo is not compelled to hoard money and is more likely to stop playing because he doesn't feel like a winner rather than because he is losing money. Leo hates to be thought of as stingy and so likes to leave generous tips. Toys and games are also ruled by Leo. Think about giving toys as presents to your adult Leos. Unusual decks of cards, a roulette wheel, or a good cribbage board are great gifts. A Leo friend told me that a new toy store had a five-story Ferris wheel in it. He was so excited that he was arranging play dates for himself and friends.

At home Leo will enjoy an armchair or piece of furniture that gives him command of the whole room. I would suggest an uncluttered decor because Leo likes to move in direct lines rather than having to make way for interesting furniture placement. Straw peacock chairs with high backs have always struck me as a particularly Leo design. Sensitivity to color is typical of Leos. Complement the usual bright vibrant colors Leo enjoys with soothing colors. A fireplace or a wood-burning stove means home to Leo.

Leo, as his symbol suggests, loves big cats, but for everyday, cats and golden-maned dogs are more reasonable. In general, a Leo wants a large dog rather than a small, yappy dog. In the same way Leo enjoys his own mane, a pet has to have beautiful fur and be well-groomed. Golden retrievers, collies, and German shepherds might particularly appeal. A Leo's home or apartment should have enough room for both dog and master. Close, cramped quarters with an animal will be uncomfortable for Leo.

Colors and Flowers

Leo is a fire sign and needs bold reds, yellows, and oranges to keep the energies vital. The current fashion for black is deadening to Leo. If you can't wean yourself from black, wear red underwear or colorful scarves. Leo takes a great deal of care in dressing well and expressing his dramatic nature in fashion. Leo loves showy, bright flowers. Dahlias, Gerberas, poppies, and peonies are all Leo flowers.

For the garden, consider giving marigolds. Trees that are especially pleasing to Leo are ash, bay, and walnut.

Metals, Gems, and Materials

Gold is the natural element of Leo and many born under this sign enjoy wearing and collecting jewelry. Leo rules the heart, and in keeping with the magnanimity of this sign, heart-shaped jewelry reminds Leos of romance and love, two of their favorite things. Most men with Leo planets wear cuff links, a gold chain or a decorative key chain. Red and yellow stones such as ruby, carnelian, citrine, and chrysolite belong to Leo. Amber is also a Leo semiprecious stone. One impeccably dressed Leo client came to me with the most intriguing red stone I have ever seen. She said it was called vulcanite. I have never seen it since but the color and sparkle epitomizes Leo's special warmth and shine.

Food, Herbs, Tastes, and Scents

All citrus, which require a good deal of sun, belong to Leo. A great gift for those in northern climates during the winter is a box of oranges or grapefruit from Florida. Leos also love the fragrance of citrus; orange water or lemon verbena could be favorite aromas. Watch and see if your Leo droops as the winter progresses. Oftentimes a light box or full spectrum bulbs can help Leo with seasonal blues.

Herbs that stimulate circulation belong to Leo and most respond well to Saint-John's-wort. Walnuts are also a wonderful gift for Leos. You may notice that there are frequently bowls of walnuts in Leos' homes. Walnut trees require good southern exposure and lots of sunlight. Walnuts are also full of omega-3 oils, which have been proven to aid those suffering depression. Tastes that are warming and slightly spicy are pleasing to Leo. Saffron, in particular, would be a good gift for a Leo cook. Flair and imagination will be the hallmarks of Leo in the kitchen. Garlic is considered an Aries spice, but most of my Leo friends and clients tell me that they love anything with garlic. One client insisted that I try her special recipe for chicken with forty cloves of garlic. It was delicious.

Travel

Travel for Leo is a chance to look at different aspects of their personality. Although Leo is a fixed sign and sometimes does not adapt to change quickly, traveling to different countries or cities gives Leos a different stage on which to experience their feelings. France might be a particular favorite with Leos; after all, it is the nation where Louis XIV, the Sun King, ruled. The pomp and ceremony that surrounded the king's waking and sleeping might try a contemporary Leo's patience, but knowing there were many people eagerly awaiting him or her is probably just the way Leo likes to feel in the morning. Other Leo destinations are Rome, the Alps, Bohemia, Bombay, and Prague.

The entire country of Italy is considered a Leo nation. In addition to the beautiful art and architecture, one of the beauties of Italy is how well put together the people are. There is a great deal of pride in making a good impression and few Italians go outside without dressing well. Leo likes this attention to fashion. Strolling on an Italian piazza or any promenade is a perfect place for Leo to see and be seen. Give travel gifts that are practical and stylish. Leo does not want to look frumpy because they are far from home.

Sports

In terms of the more physical games and sports, Leos enjoy sports that are crowd pleasers. Polo, horseback riding, and martial arts such as judo, as well as football, baseball, and basketball all appeal to Leo. Leo also like golf and golf courses. The beauty of the course is as important to them as the skill needed to play it. Leo is a very competitive sign. These natives like to win but also believe in fair play. They will never cheat or be underhanded in a contest, but they will retire from view if they lose a game. When they have stoked up their fires again, they will reappear. In sports there is a preponderance of great basketball players who are Leo. Magic Johnson, Wilt Chamberlain, and Patrick Ewing all share the sign of Leo. These players are wonderful athletes and also good showmen. Female athletes include the figure skaters Dorothy Hamill and Peggy Fleming. The great tennis player Evonne Goolagong is also a Leo. Gifts of tickets to sporting events or brightly colored exercise clothes are perfect for Leo's style.

Intellectual and Artistic Interests

The most important idea for Leos is magnanimous expression. Their pride is very strong. Leos also believe that in some way they are meant to lead. This might be in a small group of friends or in a larger sense. Their philosophical and spiritual concerns are usually based on realizing what they personally can share with people. Books about effective leadership or even a seminar in communicating would be a gift that a Leo would enjoy.

The theater usually attracts Leos and playwriting is a wonderful way for Leo to express the drama they see in life. Consider giving your Leo a subscription to the theater or a software program that enables him or her to write plays. There are a number on the market. Leos are also drawn to the visual arts, especially film and painting. They usually have an excellent sense of color and enjoy creating large canvases. I would recommend a collection of oil paints, large canvases, or a paint by number set for any Leo.

Romance

Love and romance are the fuel for Leo's life. Leos have such fun pursuing and being pursued. They are gregarious with their feelings and in romantic relationships they are very generous both with their feelings and with gifts. The sign is usually true to one person, but there may be some drama before getting to that committed partnership. Leo can be self-centered and his or her partner must realize that they need flattery and assurance to confirm their feelings about themselves. Gifts to Leos in love that would keep their fires burning would be images of stars and anything that makes them feel as if they are the center of a three-ring circus.

Well-Known Leos

When I looked at a list of well-known Leos I was struck with how many film directors there were. I think it is because Leo's leadership, performing abilities, and artistic abilities combine and are fulfilled in film. Give books about any of these directors or their films: Alfred Hitchcock, Cecil B. DeMille, Stanley Kubrick, John Huston, Lina Wertmuller, Peter Weir, Roman Polanski, Peter Bogdanovich, Ken Burns, or Blake Edwards. The painter and famous person, Andy Warhol, was also a Leo. Leos like the idea that everyone will have his or her "fifteen minutes of fame."

As Leo is the sign of the performer and one who enjoys public attention, there are many noteworthy actors and actresses to consider for gift-giving possibilities. Reruns of *I Love Lucy* with Lucille Ball or early radio or TV shows with Gracie Allen capture the humor and zaniness of this sign. One of the boldest and funniest performers of all time was the Leo Mae West. Her early films are a stitch. Contemporary Leo actresses include Sandra Bullock and Lisa Kudrow. One of the most interesting Leos to me is Martha Stewart. She reigns over an empire of homemaking creativity and has created a performance art all her own. She also has beautiful hair!

Julia Child, one of the first "performing chefs," is also a Leo.

Leo actors have a special blend of wise guy humor and intensity. Robert De Niro is a good example. In addition to his tough guy roles he has made some very funny movies. Take a look at *Analyze This*. Robert Redford is a Leo and is a leader not only as an actor and director but as an environmentalist as well. Other performers include Peter O'Toole, Dustin Hoffman, Woody Harrelson, and Martin Sheen. Ben Affleck, who is currently enjoying great success, is a Leo, as are two of the costars of *Friends*, Matt LeBlanc and Matthew Perry. Astrology is sometimes the most interesting subject because of the correspondences one finds. The great comic actor Bert Lahr was a Leo; Lahr played the cowardly lion in the film *The Wizard of Oz*. His portrayal gives a full range of Leo emotions, and of course, the character is a lion!

Rock musicians Madonna and Mick Jagger are Leo stars. In addition to their musical abilities they are both larger-than-life performers. Other popular musicians are Whitney Houston, Tori Amos, Halle Berry and the late Jerry Garcia of the Grateful Dead. The beautiful and talented singer and actress Jennifer Lopez is a Leo.

The list of Leo authors is impressive and there are many playwrights, the most famous of which is George Bernard Shaw. Shaw wrote volumes of plays with long introductions of social commentary. His two-volume biography and collected letters are fascinating. Other writers are Beatrix Potter, Alexandre Dumas (who wrote *The Count of Monte Cristo*, a fabulous summer read) and James Baldwin. Poets abound in this sign. Two of the most noteworthy poets of the Romantic era—Percy Bysshe Shelley and Alfred, Lord Tennyson—are Leos. Leo can express his or her ardor quite well, but a book of these poems might inspire them to new heights. Last, the classicist Edith Hamilton, whose translations of Greek myth have become a school standard, was a Leo. Leo loves reading about a time when kings, queens, gods, and goddesses reigned. If your Leo finds it difficult to keep track of the ancient gods and their exploits, get Edith Hamilton's *Mythology* and you will have a clear, concise compendium of Greek, Roman, and Norse myths.

Leo: Response to Celebrations and Occasions

BIRTHDAY

Leo loves being the center of attention and it probably wouldn't matter if there were presents or not just as long as everyone knows this is their day. Paper crowns, perhaps a few tiaras or playing King or Queen for a Day will make this generous fire sign feel appreciated. Try for a party outdoors if you live in a sunny climate. Leo thrives when the sun is shining.

CHRISTMAS / HANUKAH

The season of giving is tailor-made for Leo's generosity. Leo usually loves holiday parties both as a host and as a guest. Some Lions might need an extra dose of sunlight around this time but usually the warmth of holiday lights encourages a Leo's heart. Leo can easily tap into joyous childhood memories of Christmas and will enjoy playing with toys. Consider gifts such as a new game, an elegant piece of jewelry, or theater tickets.

ENGAGEMENT / MARRIAGE

An engagement gift for Leo males and females should be classic, dignified, and expensive. Popping the question is usually a dramatic event and Leo women love to describe the moment they knew that courtship was leading to marriage. Although diamonds are an Aries stone, I'd stick with a classic diamond ring for engagements. Leo men may appreciate special cuff links or a ring with a crest or symbol. Don't elope when it comes to the wedding day! Leo wants the pomp and ceremony of this special day. Not to mention it's a day to really shine. If you are giving wedding gifts to a Leo think of gifts that will stand out and be decorative. A Mixmaster won't cut it. On a deeper level, Leo entering marriage is extending his or her kingdom and will want to include all the people special to him/her. If both bride and groom are Leos, expect a heck of a party.

NEW BABY

Welcoming an infant to Leo parents is challenging because there is another person who takes over center stage. For the Leo parent, a child is an extension of self. Your gift to the baby is a gift to the parent. A humorous book on the first few months of parenting would be a welcome gift. Leo parents would also enjoy a unique birth announcement for their latest production. Surround a Leo baby with vibrant colors such as reds and yellows. A musical jack-in-the-box could keep your Leo baby occupied for hours.

NEW HOME

Home is a Leo's castle. The house should have space for entertaining and if there is an archway for an impromptu show, Leo could make use of it with home theatricals. Housewarming gifts should be noticeable. A large serving dish, a big poster, or a mural will be more appreciated than something small and delicate. Fiesta ware colors are particularly appealing to Leo.

ANNIVERSARY

A special night out with lots of flair is the best anniversary present. Both Leo men and women like to dress up. Going to a concert, show, or comedy club and then dinner will mark the occasion as special. Flashy jewelry and vibrant silk scarves are always a good gift for Leo women. Men will appreciate excellent sports equipment, and maybe even a trip to a casino.

VALENTINE'S DAY

Romance and ardor are intrinsic to Leo. The sign rules the heart and on the day that commemorates love and lovers, Leo feels buoyant and extroverted. The staple roses and chocolate suit Leo just fine. Valentine cards are apt to be humorous or even handmade. Women, don't forget that your Leo man *loves* to be praised and appreciated for his romantic attentions. Stroke his mane and you will renew your romance for another year.

MOTHER'S DAY

Spare the sentiment and go for activity. A Leo mom will enjoy anything her children give her, but a special, fun activity with everyone will be the best present. It could be going to the theater, hiking, water skiing, or a trip to a nature habitat. Leo moms love to joke around with their kids. Flowers could be roses or red azaleas or even a potted amaryllis.

FATHER'S DAY

Leo is the sign of the Father as Cancer is the sign of the Mother. Dad won't mind a colorful tie or a chance to take a special trip with just the kids. Think of the Leo father as a big-game hunter leading a safari . . . even if you just go to a local amusement park. Going out is more fun than staying home, but avoid traffic. Leo dads can be impatient and want to get where they are going rather than wading through traffic jams.

THANK-YOU PRESENT

Leos cannot stand it when someone forgets to show his or her gratitude for a party, special service, or event. You do not have to give a lavish thank-you present but forgetting to acknowledge something will be considered a serious breach in a friendship or professional relationship. Leo also will be too proud to tell you of your faux pas. You will know you've made one when the Lion passes you by. To express your thanks, consider a humorous card, or lots of multicolored balloons.

ANYTIME PRESENT

Leo always enjoys a celebrity newsmagazine or biography. Give Leo a gold star and you will feel his/her mood turn sunny. But perhaps the best anytime present is a sincere compliment about Leo's looks or accomplishments.

Leo Gift Suggestions

LEO MAN

Thrifty Saturn

Lion tie
Seven-in-one game set
Backgammon board
Roulette wheel
Bottle of Bombay Gin
Personal spotlight
Special hair products
Almonds
Guide to athletics
Book on how to write an autobiography
Yellow sneakers
Key lime pie

Luxurious Venus

Personal emblem
One diamond earring
Gold ID bracelet
Fur cap
A crown
Trip to the desert
Musk scent
Gourmet olive oil
Ornate jewelry box
A sundial
Tangerine sweater
Superman robe
Gold epaulets

A gold watch

Bountiful Jupiter

A gold mine
Racehorses
Grove of lemon trees
Gold Rolls Royce
A casino trip
Palazzo in Rome
Teak furniture
Solarium
Well-designed fireplace
A safari
A castle on a hill

LEO WOMAN

Thrifty Saturn

Almond butter
Sunburst mirror
Marigolds
Handheld bridge game
Sign saying: THRONE ROOM—AUDIENCE GRANTED BY
APPOINTMENT ONLY
Wine rack
Print of van Gogh's *Sunflowers*
Lion head drawer pulls
Rosemary
Saffron
4711 Cologne
Fuschia plant
Walnut oil

Luxurious Venus

Cat goddess bookends
Amber jewelry
Orange, red, yellow rainbow scarf
Display brackets
Brocade dressing gown
Leopard print comforter
Subscription to *Martha Stewart Living*
Linens with sun images
Costume jewelry
Hyacinth jewelry
A palomino horse
Tickets to a show
Gold-framed childhood photo

Bountiful Jupiter

An amphitheater
A showboat
Jaguar car
Desert home
A ballroom
A fur coat
Antique Christmas ornaments
Pink gold jewelry
Ruby jewelry
A sunporch
Rare wood furniture
A Broadway debut

LEO BOYS AND TEENS

Stuffed lion
Checkers/chess

Poker chips
Toy microphone
Jungle print pajamas
Baseball cards
Hawaiian shirt
Volcanic rocks
Circus tickets
Cartoon drawing kit
Pool table
Red hair dye
A roller coaster
Lottery tickets
A fun house
The Three Musketeers book, video, or comic book
Toy soldiers
A salamander
Dice
Teach yourself anything course
Parade music
Cat's eye marbles
An applause machine
A saxophone
Gold coins
Harry Potter books by Leo J. K. Rowling

LEO GIRLS AND TEENS

Cats
Sunflower jewelry
Keepsake box trimmed in gold
A gold locket
Chess set/checkers
Corduroy quilt

Lemon yellow dress
A cloak
Almond complexion soap
Sandalwood incense
Toy merry-go-round
Stuffed lion
Acting lessons
Stained-glass picture
A peacock fan
Theatrical makeup kit
Orange water cologne
An Afghan dog
Star body art/sparkle
Snow globe with a castle inside
Feather boa
Cheerleading outfit
Books on cats
Red, yellow, orange balls
A garnet ring
Tickets to a cabaret

Virgo
August 23–September 22

VIRGO
A Mutable Yin Sign

SYMBOL:	A maiden with a sheaf of wheat
RULING PLANET:	Mercury
ELEMENT:	Earth
BODY PART:	Intestines and nerves
FAVORED POSSESSIONS:	Desks with many compartments, pets, clothes with detailed patterns
COMMUNICATION STYLE:	Precise and detailed
HOME STYLE:	Organized and serene
COLORS AND METAL:	Beige, white, dark green, mercury
FOOD, PLANTS, FLOWERS:	Grains, carrots, cardamom, lilacs
PARTNERSHIP STYLE:	Reliable and considerate
RULING PASSION:	To organize thoughts so they can be effective
PHILOSOPHY:	Service to others is the way to quiet the mind
GEMSTONES:	Jasper, pearls
WISHES OR GOALS:	To create a tidy orderly world
UNCONSCIOUS DESIRE:	To revel in messiness
FOR gift-giving, KEEP IN MIND:	Virgo likes classic styles of name brand gifts.

Character Traits and Symbols

Virgo seeks perfection and purity in all endeavors. Many Virgos consult me and say with a hint of apology in their voices, "I'm a Virgo." I suspect that they are referring to the rumor that Virgos are picky, analytical, and difficult to please. I always tell Virgos that their sign characterizes the quest for perfection and that the important word is quest. If you find perfection you'll have to drop dead the next day for there will be nothing for you to do!

The essential nature of Virgo is to search for synthesis and wholeness. Their most valuable gift is the capacity for analysis and discernment. However, if Virgo relies exclusively on their critical and analytical faculties, they can become so bogged down in details that they miss the forest for the trees.

Virgo is an earth sign and the symbol is a maiden holding wheat from the harvest. The symbol harkens back to the Babylonian goddess of fertility, Ishtar. In Greek mythology, the harvest maiden was associated with Persephone, who spent six months of the year in the underworld and six months enjoying the fruits of the earth. Representations of the Virgo maiden always look like a classical statue and contemporary Virgo enjoys classical styles. Oftentimes Virgo finds a style groove and keeps it throughout life. Observe your Virgo and see what their groove is and then you know to give a gift that is familiar with a little twist. For Virgo this is continuity, not boredom. In fact, Virgo has such an active mind that they are rarely bored.

Virgo's astrological ruler is Mercury, the messenger god. Mercury rules communication and knowledge and Virgos have a thirst for knowledge that is rivaled only by Gemini, the other astrological sign ruled by Mercury. The Mercury-ruled signs are "connecting signs;" they have a quality of bringing ideas and people together. In astrology we call these signs mutable. Virgo, Gemini, Sagittarius, and Pisces are all mutable signs. The mutable signs rule when the weather is changing seasons. This changeability is why there is such great flexibility with Virgo. They are not indecisive like Libra but can see how people are thinking and adjust their attitudes accordingly. These people are wonderful and responsible employees because they can see what needs to be done and then do it. There is a great pragmatic streak to Virgo. A Virgo has a mind like a Rolodex. Ask them a question and you can almost see them sorting and categorizing in their brains until they come up with the answer to your request.

Mercury, or Hermes in Greek, was also associated with tricks and pranks. One Virgo loves to fool her

friends by sewing designer labels into very nonde-
signer items. Everyone knows she does this and has
a good laugh. Games and toys that engage the mind
tickle Virgo's sense of intricacy and humor. Word
games, books of limericks, puns, quizzes, and crossword puzzles are all very good gifts for any Virgo.
Virgo is usually a frugal sign and will not expect you
to spend a lot of money on gifts for him or her. They
may be slightly embarrassed, in fact, if you do give
them an expensive gift. If you do want to give a
luxury gift, choose something from a company or
manufacturer of long-standing and good reputation.
This pleases Virgo's sense of propriety and luxury.
Virgo would prefer Waterford crystal to a newer
brand name. Small Limoges boxes or keepsake porce-
lains are a good gift. In fashion, emphasize time-
honored designers such as Chanel, Gucci, Prada,
Brooks Brothers or Abercrombie and Fitch. Virgo
doesn't necessarily require expensive gifts but will
appreciate high quality in whatever gift you give.

If you are giving a gift to a Virgo you don't know
very well, try to find out their major interest outside
of work and give an informative book pertaining to
that interest. For example, Virgos who enjoy film and
television would enjoy a book such as *Halliwell's Film
Encyclopedia* or *Leonard Maltin's Video Guide*, which
catalogues feature films or videos and gives a synop-
sis and rating. Another possibility is a catalogue of
catalogues. Virgos enjoy searching through catalogues and having a reference catalogue would keep
a Virgo busy and happy for some time. An almanac
or historical time line book, is also a very good idea.
If you suspect the Virgo in mind has a sweet tooth,

consider an old-fashioned Whitman's Sampler. The description of the chocolates in the inside cover makes eating the candies all the more pleasurable.

Virgos like to keep things compartmentalized. One way Virgo can keep track of all their thoughts is by writing them down in a series of colored notebooks. Virgo may want to keep one for home, one for work, one for finances and one for dreams. Virgo also likes to put things in order. Containers, organizers, and closet dividers help to put physical space in order. A Virgo client of mine always works out her problems by cleaning her closets. There seems to be something cathartic for her in purging what she doesn't use anymore and making room for what is new.

Colors and Flowers

The color scheme for Virgos is of the earth. Imagine fields of grain, soft browns, navy blues, gray, pure white, black, and dark greens. Bright color is used only for accents. Country dwellers might want to plant or at least observe wildflowers. Queen Anne's lace, buttercups, sweet cicely, and Bouncing Bet are just a few examples of pleasing and interesting flowers. Virgos have the fortunate distinction of having lilac bushes under their rulership. Don't miss their brief season in May.

If you bring a bunch of flowers to your Virgo, choose white ones; Virgos love all white bouquets. In keeping with Virgo's element, earth, gardening may be a favorite activity. Gardening tools, watering cans, and special rubber shoes to keep the mud off are all accouterments that are gift possibilities for

Virgo. For urban dwellers consider window boxes with flowers such as wallflower and sweet William.

Metals, Gems, and Materials

Virgos prefer simple jewelry. Quicksilver or mercury is the metal ruled by Virgo, but outside of a thermometer it is not useful. Virgo may prefer silver or white gold to yellow gold; all agates are Virgo stones. Pearls are usually associated with the sign of Cancer, but they evoke an image of purity that is in keeping with Virgos' quest. The tradition of birthstones is varied and frequently you will see a number of different stones listed for each astrological sign. I have found that many Virgos are partial to hematite, jasper, sapphire, and chrysolite. In general Virgos prefer the "real McCoy" rather than costume jewelry; however, Virgo women often do not wear a lot of jewelry. They love getting jewelry as a gift, but don't be hurt if you don't see it on them.

Fabrics should be soft and natural. Virgo may have a special fondness for jersey or flannel. All crafts such as weaving and knitting are Virgo-ruled. Virgos are partial to yarns made with natural dyes.

Food, Herbs, Tastes, and Scents

Most Virgos are very health conscious. They usually prefer food with few spices and light sauces. Heavy cream sauces or elaborate dishes with complicated ingredients are usually too rich. Virgo can sometimes become overconcerned about health practices and diet. One Virgo woman I know has to forcibly restrain herself from reading fad diet books. She is not heavy but becomes obsessive about reading the latest diet books and broadcasting her knowledge to anyone who listens. When she is in the grip of her compulsion she finds very few people who are interested in sharing a meal with her. The solution to a Virgo who feels shaky about his or her diet is to consult a nutritionist, get a plan, and stick to it. Once a Virgo feels there is order to a problem they will relax and heal themselves.

An herb garden is perfectly suited to Virgo's health-oriented nature. Herbs that are ruled by Virgo are chicory, endive, valerian, and woodbine. For Virgos, using herbs medicinally may cut down the number of visits to the doctor.

Virgo men and women tend to have beautiful complexions. You won't go wrong in choosing colors if you keep in mind your Virgo's skin tone. In fact, a wonderful idea for a Virgo gift is a facial or special face creams. If you are a Virgo and notice that your skin is looking poorly, investigate changing your diet. Virgo rules the intestines and the way the body absorbs nutrients. This is why many people of this sign are extra careful with what they eat.

Scents for Virgos tend toward light colognes and perfumes. A strong perfume or cologne scent is unpleasant. Lavender, jasmine, bergamot and petitgrain are all possible choices for both men and women. For example, the well-known men's cologne Brut has—among other ingredients—lavender, anise, lemon, and bergamot. Chanel No. 5 has jasmine, bergamot, and neroli, in addition to other scents.

Travel

Travel for Virgo is usually well-planned and organized. Virgo has a knack for packing and loves all the little bottles and separate compartments that living on the move entails. A thoughtful gift would be a traveling drugstore. Virgo wants to have all his or her products, vitamins, medicines, herbs, etc., in one place. This sign is not really interested in exploring foreign stores for toothpaste. They know what they like and are happy to carry it with them. The most noteworthy destination ruled by Virgo is Paris. In addition to its beauty, Paris is extremely well-organized; the Métro is fast and clean and all addresses are clearly marked. Another Virgo land is Switzerland. Virgo does not enjoy chaos and travel to either Switzerland or Paris is a good choice. Other more daring possibilities are Crete, Jerusalem, Padua, and Turkey.

Sports

Sports are also a wonderful way of getting away from mental preoccupations. Tennis is ruled by Virgo. Running, track, and graceful martial arts, such as aikido, would all be sports for Virgo. Gifts related to your Virgo's sport such as a tennis towel or leg warmers would definitely be appreciated. There are many noteworthy athletes in this sign and most seem to be tennis players, runners, golfers, and baseball players. Althea Gibson was the first African-American tennis champ; Jimmy Connors was a two-time Wimbledon winner and all-time pro singles champ. Roger Maris, the first player to break Babe Ruth's single-season home run record, was a Virgo. I have it on good authority from my Sagittarian sports expert that one of the greatest players currently playing is a Virgo: Ryne Sandberg of the Chicago Cubs. My friend said, "He plays a quiet game and has redefined the position of second base." He also has played more than 100 games without an error. That may be as close to perfection as a Virgo or anyone can get. Last, the great athlete Jesse Owens was a Virgo. He won five gold medals and broke five world records in track.

Intellectual and Artistic Interests

Virgo's artistic talents are varied. Collage with paper or material is a perfect Virgo pastime. Cutting the shapes and then arranging the pieces is pleasing to Virgo's sense of order. It is an interesting exercise for anyone to use collage to help visualize something you would like or something you are trying to accomplish. Take a piece of white paper and find pictures of the house you want, the journey you'd like to take, the relationship you'd like, or whatever. Then arrange the pictures to represent what you are seeking. If you keep the collage in front of you it will remind you of the steps you can take to realize your goal.

Making pottery is also a very Virgo activity. Touching the clay and molding it is sensual and calming. Virgo rules all sewing and handicrafts. Twin sisters I know with Virgo moons are never without a piece of embroidery or needlework in their hands.

It sounds quaint in this age of electronic gadgets but these ladies find the handwork pleasurable. Virgo must keep his or her mind engaged or they can obsessively worry about small details. Giving gifts that encourage Virgo to do creative work is the best antidote to this tendency.

Intellectually the single most important gift for a Virgo could be a library card. Virgo likes to read and the peace and order of libraries also appeal. The sign is very interested in gathering information. One Virgo, who later went on to be a librarian, collected dictionaries just for the pleasure of looking up foreign words.

In terms of beliefs, Virgo tends to be conservative. The saying "God is in the details" could be considered Virgo's creed. Service or doing good works is an important component in their spiritual practice.

Romance

Traditionally, Virgo was called the sign of the bachelor or spinster. I have not done any statistical analysis on this fact and most Virgos I know have a partner; however, the sign does not gush over romance. Virgo men are considerate and consistent and Virgo women are the same. Part of Virgo's character is a strong sense of service and in love these people believe if they have made a commitment that they are honor bound to follow through. The sign usually does not date a lot and is very choosy with whom they become intimate. Virgos can easily tidy up their feelings. This characteristic can be an asset, as sometimes we have to get on with life no matter how we feel. It can become a liability in intimate relationships since Virgo's are known for turning cold on a dime. The most important thing for Virgos in love to remember is "touch first, think later." If Virgo can keep in contact with his feelings, he will not get lost in debating or criticizing his partner's strengths and weaknesses. Couple's massage and a large enough bathtub for two would be perfect for a Virgo in a relationship.

Well-Known Virgos

There are a large number of well-known Virgo writers. Two major geniuses were Leo Tolstoy and Johann Wolfgang von Goethe. Tolstoy's novel *War and Peace* is, in my opinion, the pinnacle of literary achievement. It takes a while to get all the Russian names straight but it is a great book and a great gift. Goethe was a poet, playwright, and scientist. In addition to his beautiful plays *Faust*, Part I and Part II, his theory of colors meticulously examined the study of color and light. More recent authors include O. Henry, D. H. Lawrence, Richard Wright, and Agatha Christie, whose mysteries may appeal to the Virgo love of intricacy. Mary Shelley, the author of *Frankenstein*, was a Virgo. The beauty of this story is the pure feelings of the misunderstood monster. Consider giving the book or a video of the classic film.

Virgo has its share of excellent performers. As I mentioned before, the sign has a reputation for being hesitant about the opposite sex. Virgos Sophia Loren, Greta Garbo, Ingrid Bergman, Lauren Bacall, Anne

Bancroft, and Cameron Diaz clearly refute this notion. All beautiful women and wonderful actresses, they have the translucent quality that I associate with Virgo. Sophia Loren once said she owed her figure to spaghetti—an interesting tribute to Virgo's rulership of wheat and the harvest!

Actors born under the sign of Virgo have enormous appeal. My personal favorite is the first Bond, James Bond, or Sean Connery. Connery went on to do countless other roles but the James Bond films are an excellent way for Virgo to relax the busy mind. Peter Sellers is another wonderful example of precise and humorous acting. His many comedy roles, such as the three different characters in *Dr. Strangelove*, are so clearly etched that it is difficult to tell they are the same person. Good-looking and skilled Virgo actors include Richard Gere, Jeremy Irons, and Hugh Grant.

There are quite a few well-known film directors born under Virgo. Most notable are Elia Kazan, who brought incredible passion and realism to the screen; Richard Attenborough, director of the film *Gandhi*; and Robert Wise, director of *West Side Story*. An artist draws on many parts of the personality, but all these directors have a definite eye for detail and created memorable films. Virgo, as I mentioned before, likes to know the details of any subject. If you give your Virgo a video of any of these artists, include a biography or film history that relates some of the background for each artist. Better yet, buy them a DVD, since these usually include enormous amounts of additional information about the film.

Gifts for music connoisseurs could be CDs by Debussy, Bruckner, and Pachelbel. Pachelbel's *Canon* became a piece frequently used in exercise and yoga classes because it is so calm. As a pick-me-up, consider music by the Virgo Jelly Roll Morton, a ragtime composer whose composition "The Entertainer" is now well-known from the film *The Sting*. Another wonderful Virgo musician was Leonard Bernstein. In addition to his beautiful music, Bernstein's lectures on the history of music are informative and very entertaining. The King of Pop, Michael Jackson, is a Virgo. Listen to him, watch him dance, read about his life. He is a fascinating personality and a perfectionist in all things.

One of the attributes of Virgo is that it is the sign of service. There are some noteworthy personalities who have given the world extraordinary service and their writings or life stories would provide inspiration for any Virgo. First is Mother Teresa, the nun who devoted her life to serving India's poor. Also a Virgo is Maria Montessori, the founder of a gentle method of educating kids who wrote extensively about child development and education.

Virgo: Response to Celebrations and Occasions

BIRTHDAY

Virgo enjoys telling people their age. No doubt because they often look younger than their years. I also think Virgo enjoys reviewing the details of past birthdays. These people are flexible and will enjoy a surprise party, a private dinner, or a hamburger at the ball game. Virgo also can be content if they have to spend a birthday alone. Virgo is rarely bored and if they spend a day alone they know that people will come into their lives the next day.

CHRISTMAS / HANUKAH

Service is a key word for Virgo and many people of this sign may make an extra effort to do some charity work or volunteer service during the holidays. Virgo needs to watch holiday eating and drinking as the system can be susceptible to digestive discomforts. Virgo may be happier giving presents than receiving them. Please your Virgo, male or female, with a relaxation treat of a facial, massage, or spa day.

ENGAGEMENT

Virgo women will know very clearly whether they want to marry and whether they will accept a proposal. If you are proposing to a Virgo, you have the best chance of success by asking simply in lovely surroundings. A classic diamond engagement ring is the most pleasing. Engagement parties for both bride and bridegroom will be successful if they are well-organized. Choose name brands for crystal and china. Also remember that Virgo is an earth sign and may like pottery or ceramic dishes.

MARRIAGE

Virgo brides and grooms will think out every detail of their wedding. The beginning of life together is the start of a cooperative enterprise where the division of labor will be tidy and effective. Give Virgos useful gifts that look good. A Virgo couple will not mind two Mixmasters. It will come in handy if one breaks.

NEW BABY

A Virgo baby can be fussier than other children until they get their eating plan under control. A white-noise machine for the bedroom would be a soothing and welcome present. Keep colors in the baby's room pastel and the lighting soft. Virgo babies have a sensitive system. For a Virgo parent any gift that gives information about parenting would be welcome. I would specially recommend any of the "how to get baby to sleep" books as well as books on nutrition.

NEW HOME

Virgo runs a tight ship. The home will usually be neat and have a quiet order. An interesting present would be a large vase with a sheaf of wheat or other ornamental grasses. Virgo's symbol is the maiden carrying grain from the harvest. More traditional presents such as earthenware pottery or an index file for recipes would also be appreciated. For male Virgo households choose gifts in monochromatic colors: white, black, beige, or earth tones.

ANNIVERSARY

Many Virgos would enjoy a special trip to commemorate an anniversary. The sign is usually not sentimental, so you don't have to re-create the scene of your wedding or honeymoon, but going somewhere interesting will make a lasting impression. Also, since Virgos tend to be plan-makers, the best gift may be for the non-Virgo partner to take over the social plans and arrangements for an anniversary.

VALENTINE'S DAY

Virgo, being a sensual earth sign, wants to touch on Valentine's Day. A massage or facial could be more appreciated than the traditional flowers and chocolate. Virgo has sensitive digestion and may not care for sweets. White flowers are more pleasing than red. Also, Virgo may not care to go out on the holiday. A private celebration is more in keeping with the shy side of Virgo.

MOTHER'S DAY

Virgo mothers have a plan for parenting and are usually very thorough. A special treat would be for the kids and Dad to plan the day for Mom. Take her to the ballet, a show, or a concert. Maybe there is an exhibition of quilts or handicrafts in the area? The fact that someone else planned the day will be as much a gift as the excursion.

FATHER'S DAY

Virgo fathers pride themselves on their intellectual curiosity and knowledge. A perfect gift for Dad would be an encyclopedia or almanac on some of his favorite subjects. Virgo dads may also be sportsmen.

A new tennis racquet or other equipment would be a perfect opportunity for family fun.

Thank-You Present

For Virgo, a heartfelt thank-you may be enough. The words are important, and since frequently Virgo does not enjoy clutter, they may not expect a present for every occasion. A thoughtful gift would be a beautiful coffee table book or monogrammed stationery.

Anytime Present

Virgo won't mind at all if you give them coupons that you found for products you know he or she uses. Choose practical presents that make life easier. Virgo also has an interest in herbs and face creams. A small bottle of an herbal facial or body lotion is an excellent anytime present. The sign loves to learn and a book about an unknown subject is always a good choice.

Virgo Gift Suggestions

VIRGO MAN

Thrifty Saturn

Garden tools
100 sharp pencils
An atlas
Mahogany remote control holder
A Buddy Holly CD
Dictionary of slang
White polo shirt
Navy blue slacks
Edge trimmer
Subscription to *Consumer Reports*
A massage
Worry beads

Luxurious Venus

Fitted white shirts
Handmade clothing
Jasper ring
Thick Turkish towels
A juicer
Beehives
Palm Pilot
Rolltop desk
A rocking chair
Trip to Crete
Monogrammed handkerchiefs
A global positioning system

Bountiful Jupiter

Fields of wheat
Swiss skiing trip
An apartment in Paris
A home library
A Volvo
Pedigree dogs
A barn
Personal streetcar
Mont Blanc pen
Private tennis court

VIRGO WOMAN

Thrifty Saturn

Lilacs
Wheat grass juice
Lavender talc
A massage
Malt balls
Flower note cards
Coupon holder
Book of herbal remedies
Ivory pashmina scarf
Worry beads
Gardening gloves
White gloves
Portable file cabinet

Luxurious Venus

Jute rug
Apothecary chest

Curio cabinet
Caned-back chairs
Bamboo garden furniture
A trip to Switzerland
Crystal perfume bottles
Armani beige suit
Cashmere dress coat
Facial gift subscription

Bountiful Jupiter

A trip to the Virgin Islands
Cinnabar jewelry
Daily delivery of white roses
Ivory damask bed linens
Ornamental bird cages
A trip to Los Angeles
Shaker furniture
A butler
Health spa vacation
Personal trainer
Mahogany bookcases
String of pearls

VIRGO BOYS AND TEENS

Cliffs Notes
A puppy
Birdhouse
Whistles
A hamster
Ivory sweater
A compass
A maze

Crossword puzzle books
Etch-A-Sketch
Ping-Pong table
Encyclopedia
Tennis racquet
Mathematical games
Chinese checkers
A toy chest
Foreign language translator
Handwriting analysis
Stuffed toy dogs or cats
Book of limericks
White sneakers
Blazer with insignia
Mechanical toys
A bookshelf with secret compartments
Clay or Play-Doh

VIRGO GIRLS AND TEENS

Blue-eyed cats
Facial masks
Stuffed toy squirrel
Lavender soap
Miniature tea set
Whistle key ring
Colored pencils
Sewing kit
Embroidery thread
Personal notebooks
Calligraphy pen
Decorative boxes
Set of porcelain figurines

Popsicle sticks for craft projects
Lavender bath salts
A white robe
CD of different accents
Bureau with many compartments
A date book
Origami paper
Pink jasper
Puzzle ring
Flannel pajamas
Paper dolls
Miss Manners books

Libra
September 23–October 22

LIBRA
A Cardinal Yang Sign

SYMBOL:	The Scales
RULING PLANET:	Venus
ELEMENT:	Air
BODY PART:	Kidneys and adrenal glands
FAVORED POSSESSIONS:	Silk anything, jewelry, or pieces of art
COMMUNICATION STYLE:	Indecisive and fair
HOME STYLE:	Beautiful and luxurious
COLORS AND METALS:	Pastel greens and blues, copper, brass, bronze
FOOD, PLANTS, FLOWERS:	Bonbons, berries, apple trees, roses
PARTNERSHIP STYLE:	Idealistic and eager to please
RULING PASSION:	To create personal and social harmony
PHILOSOPHY:	Go to extremes to find the middle way
GEMSTONES:	Opal
WISHES OR GOALS:	The world should be beautiful and balanced.
UNCONSCIOUS DESIRE:	To express anger directly
FOR GIFT-GIVING, KEEP IN MIND:	Libra likes beautiful things rather than practical ones.

Character Traits and Symbols

Libra is the sign of partnership and marks the beginning of the soul's consideration of others. The personality is developed from Aries through Virgo, and beginning with the sign of Libra the soul begins its journey toward harmony with others and society. The word "we" comes to their lips more easily than "I." Librans can be as egotistical as other signs, but they think of life in terms of relationships and sometimes in their zeal mistakenly assume that their personal preferences are always enjoyable to their partners. Libra's goal is balance but can become unbalanced easily because they frequently see all sides of a question, and the consideration of so many possibilities leads to conflicts of opinion within themselves. This conflict gives rise to the famous Libran indecision. The best course of action is Socrates' golden rule: "everything in moderation." When Libra's scales are balanced between thought and action they usually make the right decision.

Libra's symbol is the Scales, which represent the need for balance and harmony—the hallmark of this social sign. Interestingly enough, Libra is the only sign of the zodiac whose symbol is an inanimate object. The Libran can sometimes feel detached and superior to the scrambling, chaotic feelings of other people. At its best, this tendency gives a great ability to judge fairly and fight for equality between people. At its worst, the Libran remains aloof and condescending toward others. However, there is such charm with dimples and smiles in most Librans that people tend to forgive them their snobbishness.

The planet Venus is Libra's ruler and Venus (Aphrodite in the Greek myths) was the goddess who beguiled men and gods alike. She was laughter loving and was said to have sprung from the foam of the sea. If you look at Botticelli's painting *The Birth of Venus*, or "Venus on the half shell" as it is colloquially called, you will have a good image of the goddess. The Romans said of her "without her there is no joy nor loveliness anywhere." Other myths state that Venus is treacherous and malicious and exerts a deadly destructive power over men. Two parts of the Libran personality are described in these myths. The superficial heartbreaker who trifles with people's feelings and the gracious, generous partner who shares his or her joy with everyone. As you might suspect, many Librans are busy balancing these extremes in their personalities.

It is interesting to note that Libra, in astrology, is a masculine or yang sign. There is grit and determination beneath the charm and smiles. Libra is called the steel hand in the velvet glove. Women of this sign can be very tough and politically minded. While they are often leaders and the breadwinners of the family, Libra men have an aesthetic part of their nature, which defines their character. One Libran man, who was a business leader, told me that he wasn't at all comfortable if he had to go into a store or restaurant that wasn't tastefully decorated. In Jungian terms the male animus is strong in Libra women; and the female anima is strong in Libra men.

As an air sign, Libra is involved with matters of intellect and communication. The other air signs are Gemini and Aquarius. Gemini's mental orientation is generally for the intrinsic pleasure of experiencing many different ideas. Aquarians focus their thinking on ideas that benefit friends and society. Librans think about others in order to understand themselves and relationships. The motivation for someone's action is frequently more important to them than the act itself. Librans can be skillful psychologists but must learn to keep a firm sense of their own center; otherwise, in their attempt to understand they lose their own viewpoint. Their airy thoughts can become very involved with figuring out the best strategy to use to achieve their personal goals. Sometimes the Libran spends an inordinate amount of time game-planning and trying to control every contingency. Typically, in trying to figure out some intention or dynamic in a relationship, a Libran will think, "Well, if he does this, then I will do this, but maybe if he does that, I won't have to do this." It can be exhausting and the best course of action is to take a walk in the fresh air or sit down and calm the either/ or tendency of the mind to make difficulties. If you

are the partner or friend of a Libran, it is best not to
interfere with this mental whirl. You will only add
new variables.

Venus also rules luxury, gifts, and giving in general. This sign is tremendously aware of the nuance
of meaning in giving gifts and keeping the balance
concerning what is an appropriate gift for each type
of relationship. You may find that Libra keeps a mental account of spending for each person on his or her
list so that no person feels favored or slighted. As a
gift receiver, Libra will be happy with any and all
gifts, especially if they are decorative and appeal to
their aesthetic sense. Do not make the mistake of giving a gift such as an eggbeater because your Libran
wife mentioned she needed one or a pair of socks
because your husband's sock drawer is low—that is,
unless the eggbeater is a special Italian design and
harmonizes with all the colors in the kitchen and the
socks are a silk-and-wool blend that match perfectly
with the sweater you were planning to buy.

Libra certainly enjoys luxury but you don't necessarily have to spend a lot to keep a smile on your
Libran's face. The most important aspect is that the
gift expresses your feelings. Libra, after all, is the sign
of relationships.

Colors and Flowers

Color is very important to Libra. Choose pastels in
cool tones rather than hot colors. Lavender, blue, cool
green, and white are good colors for Libra. In warm
tones, choose pinks, peachy colors, and pale yellow.
A splash of intense color such as a scarf or jacket

works, but it shouldn't be too wild; Librans seek balance even in their wardrobe. One Libran lawyer wore the most colorful print ties with his three-piece suits.

Libra has an affinity with orderly gardens and space that is harmonious. A garden of many different colored flowers is not as pleasing as neat rows of color. Roses are a Libran flower and always a good gift. I don't recommend red roses; lighter pinks, yellow or small peach tea roses are the colors Librans most enjoy. All flowers are ruled by Venus and Libra particularly enjoys gladiolas, roses, violets, and hydrangeas. I know one man who sent a flower arrangement to his Libran wife every fifteenth of the month. This was a wonderful gift that spoke to Libra's love of flowers and marriage. Fruit trees are Libra-ruled. Groves of peach trees or grapevines would be a perfect place to take a Libra on a picnic.

Metals, Gems, and Materials

If you imagine the fire flecks in opals, the gemstone most associated with Libra, you can understand something about the Libran temperament as well as choosing a wonderful gift. The pale blue or milky opal looks placid and calm, but when you study the stone, there are flashes of darting fiery color that quickly change. Most Librans love jewelry and the legend that opals are lucky for Librans seems to be true. One Libran woman I know inherited her mother's opals and many opportunities seemed to open up for her after that. Librans don't mind wearing jewelry to the grocery store or the post office. Men are apt to wear cuff links, rings, and tiepins. Although out of fashion, a watch chain and pocket watch would not be strange to a Libran man. Rich blue sapphires, green emeralds and chrysolite are also stones that Libra enjoys. Any of these stones in an antique setting is a perfect gift for your Libra.

The metals copper and brass are associated with the sign of Libra. One Libra client has copper-topped tables throughout her house. I notice that she frequently taps the table as if to caress the copper. Jewelry made from gold and platinum is also appreciated, but if you can find higher-carat gold like eighteen or twenty-two, which tend to have a rosy patina, it would make a lovely present.

Silk is the fabric of choice for Librans. Consider giving your Libran silk long underwear to wear all winter. Any gift for a Libran man or woman that is made from silk is sure to be a hit. Other materials associated with Libra are ribbons and lace. A lovely wedding gift for a Libra would be some antique lace. I noticed a canopy of ribbons in a Libran's bedroom once and wondered if she knew how true to her sign she was being.

Food, Herbs, Tastes, and Scents

Each sign rules a part of the body; Libra rules the kidneys and adrenals. These organs keep the entire body's energy system balanced. Herbs or fruit that are beneficial for the kidneys are chamomile and cranberries. Balance in diet is important for Libra. It is a tad too easy for many of this sign to put on weight or overindulge in sweets. Liqueurs and fancy drinks with parasols delight Libra's taste and eye but tart drinks are probably better for the system. The gift of a box of marzipan or macaroons would be a special treat. Rather than drinking coffee, the Chinese herb combination of ginseng and royal bee jelly is an excellent pick-me-up for Libra. Drinking enough water and sleeping are the two most important parts of Libra's health regime. People in this sign need a lot of sleep and don't do well without it. All sweetly scented perfumes, soaps, and bath oils delight the Libran. Vanilla, almond scent, and the perfume Shalimar would all please a Libra.

Travel

Travel is usually a favorite activity for Libra because of the opportunity to see so many beautiful sights and to shop. Men and women alike enjoy poking in bazaars or markets in a foreign country. China is Libra-ruled. In Chinese culture and astrology, there are five elements, rather than the four we have in the West. Librans may be particularly interested in reading up on this system before they visit China. Other countries that resonate with Libra are Tibet, Argentina, Austria, Egypt, and Japan. These places are not the only options but wherever Libra goes, they prefer civilized travel to camping in the wild or being uncomfortable. Any place with a first-class hotel would probably be very pleasant. Vienna, with its gracious old buildings and pastry shops filled with tempting cream delights, seems to me the epitome of a Libran city. Other Libra destinations are Antwerp, Frankfurt, and Lisbon. A thoughtful gift would be durable yet attractive traveling clothes. Wherever Libra goes he or she wants to look good.

Sports

Sports that interest Libra must have a touch of elegance about them. Tennis, golf, and maybe even polo would be the activities that Librans gravitate to. Librans usually have a great deal of physical grace and enjoy sports that require sustained fluid movement. There is a hidden aggression in Libra. Too polite to express, it is best to give it an outlet through sports; martial arts may be particularly appealing. Men and women usually wear coordinated, colorful clothes for exercising or casual wear. A Libran's T-shirt will match their slacks or shorts. They will also appreciate T-shirts with tasteful designs or slogans. The current vogue for "in your face" messages on T-shirts would not be a prized gift for a Libra. Outward appearance and how others see them is a vital part of this most relationship oriented sign.

Well-known sports figures are underrepresented in Libra but three are noteworthy. Probably the most well-known was the great ballplayer Mickey Mantle. In addition to his athletic success he began a successful chain of restaurants. Contemporary athletes, the great tennis player Martina Navratilova and the famous San Fransisco 49ers wide receiver Jerry Rice are also Librans.

Intellectual and Artistic Interests

Gifts that appeal to the Libran's intellectual interests are always appreciated but the gifts must be intrinsically aesthetic. Aquarius might enjoy a set of books on philosophy and not care particularly whether they are beautifully bound; the Libran wants beauty as well as knowledge. Leather-bound books or illustrated books are great gift ideas. Many adult Librans still appreciate children's books, especially classics with illustrations. The single most important idea to a Libran is fairness. A pair of antique scales or a statue of Justice holding the scales might be a wonderful gift for your Libran.

Venus is the patron goddess of the arts. Most Librans are talented in one or more artistic activities. One client makes the most beautiful abstract color pencil drawings just to relax her brain. Librans usually have performing ability but many may be too shy to sing. Playing musical instruments or acting would be the most likely performing outlets. Consider giving the gift of a music lesson or a subscription to the symphony. Libra gets a lot of practice writing because the sign invariably writes thank-you notes for gifts or kindnesses received. With just a little more imagination, writing stories, poems, and essays could be a wonderful hobby. Books or artistic kits that encourage creativity would always be a welcomed gift.

Romance

The Libran, male or female, in love is a happy camper. Romance and all the intricacies of relationships make the Libran glow with anticipated pleasure. The men are gentlemen and pay attention to little things like flowers and candy. The women are ladies and find out their mate's preferences. They will be happy to wear the shoes he likes or cook his favorite meals. Both Libra men and women may be profligate in the spending department.

As their symbol implies, Librans' need for balance extends to how they communicate with their lover, spouse, or friend. Always seeking balance, they're likely to play devil's advocate. If someone says, "So and so is a conceited prig," the Libran may respond, "No, he isn't. He just thinks highly of himself." There is a tendency to balance all communication by re-phrasing the statement in a less critical manner and having the last word. Libra also tend to offer solutions and arguments rather than understanding a person's feelings. Librans without water in their charts may be accused of not being empathetic. There is a detachment that can be maddening. This comes from a need for harmony. They fear strong emotion because of the disruption it brings. All Librans need to work on not idealizing love so they can truly see who their partner is and not constantly compare them to the man or woman of their dreams. It might be tough, as Libra secretly believes he or she is the epitome of romance, and therefore, whomever they choose is worthy of their ideal of love. Luckily, most Librans believe in long-standing marriages and will choose to spend a lot of time pursuing their ideals.

Well-Known Librans

The list of well-known Librans is considerable and focused primarily in the arts. There are, however, a number of politicians and leaders who are Librans.

One of the most interesting people was Gandhi. His inspirational writings on nonviolent political action reflect both the force of Libra and Librans' dislike of open conflict. Margaret Thatcher, the Iron Lady, is a Libra. You find a steely will coupled with a proper white-glove-wearing lady. It was an effective combination during the time she was prime minister. Jimmy Carter, another Libra, was a very interesting president. Historians will debate the merits of his presidency but his greatest contribution seems to be in his current work as an international diplomat and peacekeeper and in his work with Habitat for Humanity. Other noteworthy political figures are the playwright and president of Czech Republic, Václav Havel; Eleanor Roosevelt; and Jesse Jackson. Biographies of all of these people would interest Librans, as they love to read and are fascinated by individuals' relationships to power. Don't miss the epic film of Gandhi's life. It is an inspiration.

A number of well-known Librans are writers. Gifts of books or plays by these authors will appeal to Libra's sense of aesthetics and artistry. The classic *Don Quixote* was written by the Libran Miguel de Cervantes. Don Quixote's valiant search for adventure to please his mythical Lady Dulcinea illustrates the idealism and devotion to romance of many Librans. The book is wonderful; there is also a television version, with Libran John Lithgow, and of course, the musical *Man of La Mancha*. Other classic authors include the Latin poet Virgil, Friedrich Nietzsche, and Oscar Wilde—all born on the same day. Take your Libran to Wilde's play *The Importance of Being Earnest* or watch the movie. It is probably the funniest play in the English language. Two of America's greatest playwrights, Arthur Miller and Eugene O'Neill, are Librans. The writers William Faulkner and T. S. Eliot were Libran and Nobel Prize winners. Contemporary Libran writers are Anne Rice, the late Mario Puzo, and Thomas Wolfe. These authors' books, movies made from the books, biographies, etc., would all be rich considerations for gifts.

Two of the major actresses of the nineteenth century, Sarah Bernhardt and Eleonora Duse, were both Librans. These two women used very different acting styles but both were incredible artists. There are many biographies of Sarah Bernhardt as well as a few film clips of her work. Duse toured America in the 1920s. A biography of Duse called *The Mystic in the Theatre* is fascinating reading for all theater people. The list of twentieth-century actresses is also significant. Gwyneth Paltrow, Kate Winslet, Neve Campbell, Julie Andrews, Helen Hayes, Deborah Kerr, Brigitte Bardot, and Lillian Gish are a few. If you are familiar with these actresses, you may notice they all have the Libran smile.

Noteworthy Libran actors are Christopher Reeve, Michael Douglas, Yves Montand, Marcello Mastroianni, and Montgomery Clift. George C. Scott was one of the most versatile Libran actors. His performances in *Dr. Strangelove* and *Patton* are unforgettable. Writer and actor Matt Damon is a Libran who well illustrates the sign's multiple talents. Film and astrology buffs might like to ponder the fact that Charlton Heston, Susan Sarandon, and Buster Keaton were all Librans born on the same day.

Vladimir Horowitz, the great pianist, was a Libra. There is something so elegant and refined in his playing that it epitomizes the balanced effortlessness that is Libra's gift. In addition to giving gifts of his CDs, you can find filmed versions of some of his concerts. The great tenor Luciano Pavarotti is also a Libran; any of his records would make an excellent gift choice. In a more popular vein Patsy Cline and Laura Nyro are Libran singers. John Lennon was a Libra; his partnership with Paul McCartney was one of the most fruitful relationships in rock history.

Libra: Response to
Celebrations and Occasions

BIRTHDAY

A Libra's birthday is an opportunity to have a party for their entire social circle, and being social is what Libra is all about. The party may be more important than the birthday. As mentioned, Libra is extremely sensitive to the underlying intention or meaning of gifts and may greet birthdays with a sense of trepidation: Will the present speak to him or her? The best choice is to look for something well-designed, beautiful, and colorful. Men might enjoy a set of colored casual shirts and women a set of matching shoes and bag.

CHRISTMAS/HANUKAH

The social aspect of the holidays can wear down even a Libra's appetite for parties. If your Libra likes to put a lot of effort into holiday plans the best gift might be a caterer, cleaning service, or a gift certificate for these services. As for an actual present, choose gifts that are luxurious. Libra wants comfort and to be spoiled at holiday time. Librans also want to share holidays with their partner.

ENGAGEMENT/MARRIAGE

Libra is in love with all phases of partnership. Engagement and marriage are the big events for most Librans. Presents should be classic and connected to some family tradition. If you give a shower for a Libra bride, forget the custom of risqué jokes or innuendo. Librans do not enjoy "dirty talk." Although stag parties are going out of fashion, most Libra men will not appreciate a big bash at the local strip joint. Whichever partner is the Libra will most probably determine the taste and style of the home. What matters for Libra in marriage is companionship; thus, in addition to gifts for the home, books on "cooking for two" or romantic hideaways would be thoughtful presents. The joy of life for Libra is keeping a marriage vital and romantic.

NEW BABY

Libra parents may feel overwhelmed by the chaos a new baby brings. A thoughtful gift would be to pay for a nurse or a nanny for the first few weeks. For Libra babies, choose pastel colors for both boys and girls. Musical mobiles may be especially appreciated. Libra babies startle easily and can pick up any dissent in the atmosphere. Music is very calming to them. Although Mozart was an Aquarius, his music would still soothe a Libra infant.

NEW HOME

A new home for a Libra is like a painter's canvas. The infinite possibilities engage their love of design. Gifts should be practical and decorative. Libra men and women like things to be matching. Table linens, sheets, and towels should all be in harmonious colors. Lightly scented candles may be a particularly favorite gift.

ANNIVERSARY

A very special day that will usually be well-celebrated even if there have been fights and tension in the relationship two days before. Both Libra men and women want to go out. A special dinner, trip to the museum, walk in a garden, or shared sporting event would be perfect. The important element is harmony. This is the day that began your partnership and no matter what stresses and strains exist, it is holy to you.

VALENTINE'S DAY

Libra loves romance and will certainly appreciate the traditional gifts of chocolate and flowers, but there is an eccentric streak in Libra that would really go for some unique trinket or personal gift to commemorate love. Think about a fire opal in its uncut state; it's not expensive and it is Libra's birthstone. Having this opal on the desk or bureau would be a touchstone for a Libra.

MOTHER'S DAY

A Libra mom is very aware of how she and her children look. Social impressions are important. She would prefer to go out than have dinner at home and would *love* it if all her children dressed up and forfeited jeans and sneakers for one day. Gifts such as perfume and jewelry are typical but always appreciated.

FATHER'S DAY

Libra dads (in fact, most Libra men) are usually very good-looking and won't mind at all a present that complements their looks. Fitted shirts might be a good idea. If the kids want to take Dad out, make it a special restaurant. Libra wants an atmosphere of comfort and some sophistication. If your dad is an opera lover, consider giving him some CDs by the Libra Luciano Pavarotti.

GRADUATION

Librans may feel sentimental about leaving the old school but will also eagerly look forward to the many new relationships the next phase of life will hold. Autograph books, scrapbooks, or a gold frame for the diploma are excellent gifts to contain Libra's memories. Remember the party celebrating the event is half the fun.

THANK-YOU PRESENT

First off, some kind of acknowledgment or thanks is essential for a Libra host or hostess. Libra is very big on manners and you may not be asked back if you forget yours. A note or e-mail is expected. If you want to give a gift in thanks for a dinner or some favor choose something small and colorful. Libra loves to do favors for people and also loves to be acknowledged for doing them. The sign is a considerate friend and will always reciprocate for dinners and parties.

ANYTIME PRESENT

Flowers are a perfect anytime present for both men and women. Libra usually enjoys something pretty or attractive rather than useful. The best present is a date to go out and enjoy something together. Libra likes it best when an experience is shared.

Libra Gift Suggestions

LIBRA MAN

Thrifty Saturn

Hammock for two
Dried apricots
A lucky rabbit's foot
Crimson sweater
An easel
Guitar music
John Lennon CDs
Rosewood box
Multicolored pens
Almond clusters
Leather driving gloves

Luxurious Venus

Copper fountain
White marble sculpture
Book on how to make decisions
Silk pastel colored ties
A tailored suit
Leather bound copy of *Don Quixote*
Oriental prints
Golf clubs
Sky blue sweater
A muffler
Cherry wood cigar humidor
Plush carpeting

Bountiful Jupiter

A mountain retreat
A dovecote
Oriental rug
Personal limousine
A Bentley
Jade incense burners
A home decorated in pastel colors
A formal garden
Opal cuff links
Paintings by classical artists
A white marble Cupid

LIBRA WOMAN

Thrifty Saturn

Spice jars
Washable silk slip
Specialty honey
Bride magazine
Black cherry preserves
Perfume bottle with jonquil scent
Tape of birdsong
Napkin rings
Organza gift bags
Embroidered pillowcases
Fruit plates
A picnic basket
Tea for two

Luxurious Venus

St. Francis garden sculpture

Marble pedestal
Silk sheets
Pink silk pajamas
Brass candlesticks
Opal ring
Silk drawstring purse
A boutique filled with silk scarves
Statue of Venus
Cloisonné boxes
Lapis lazuli jewelry

Bountiful Jupiter

A rose garden
Trip to Tibet
Trip to Japan
Chinchilla coat
Siamese cats
Cherry wood bedroom set
Black opal ring
Symphony orchestra playing Gershwin's "Rhapsody in Blue"
Carved mahogany chest
A white Porsche
Set of Wedgwood china

LIBRA BOYS AND TEENS

Music lessons
Paint by numbers kit
Cotton candy
Pale green shirt
A seesaw
Ouija board

A music box
A brass scale
A coral earring
A forest ranger hat
Juggling balls
Quartz crystal
Oscar Wilde's plays
Butterscotch sundaes
Badminton equipment
Airplane models
Pastels
Solitaire game
An abacus
An attic hideaway
Book of children's poetry
Tibetan shirt
Birdwatching books
Bubble machine
Mickey Mantle memorabilia
Mountain bike

LIBRA GIRLS AND TEENS

Ballet clothes
Pink diary
Ribbons
Barbie doll
Learn-to-draw kit
Dress-up trunk
Stuffed toy—white kitten
An Easter bonnet
Pink pajamas
A cameo ring

Lavender accent pillows
Pansies
Mary Poppins CD
Matching lacy nightgown and robe
Skating skirt
Advice for teens on party-giving
A musical jewelry box
A theatrical makeup mirror
Love poetry books
Rose bath salts
Pink zircon ring
Two heart-shaped boxes
A dressing table
White cottontail
Green leather gloves

Scorpio
October 23–November 21

SCORPIO
A Fixed Yin Sign

SYMBOL:	The Scorpion, the Eagle, and the Phoenix
RULING PLANETS:	Mars and Pluto
ELEMENT:	Water
BODY PART:	Reproductive and elimination organs
FAVORED POSSESSIONS:	A locked box, a magnifying glass, clear crystal
COMMUNICATION STYLE:	Secretive and sarcastic
HOME STYLE:	Private and dark
COLORS AND METALS:	Maroon and black, plutonium and iron
FOOD, PLANTS, FLOWERS:	Caviar, garlic, hawthorn, rhododendron, calla lilies
PARTNERSHIP STYLE:	Loyal and passionate
RULING PASSION:	Passion and power
PHILOSOPHY:	Going through the dark parts of life brings light
GEMSTONES:	Onyx, garnet
WISHES OR GOALS:	To penetrate the mysteries of life
UNCONSCIOUS DESIRE:	To be possessed
FOR GIFT-GIVING, KEEP IN MIND:	Scorpio has a wicked sense of humor and likes mysterious gifts.

♏

Character Traits and Symbols

The mysterious sign of Scorpio is the strongest sign of the zodiac. This strength lies in the amount of creative passion the sign has available to command.

In mythology Pluto, Scorpio's ruler, was the god of the Underworld. He was a fierce god but also one deeply connected to the power, fecundity, and riches of the earth. Pluto in Latin means "the rich one." The riches of Scorpio may not always be material but these very magnetic people always have the strength and focus to re-create themselves no matter what difficulties come their way. In Greek mythology Pluto's name was Hades. One of Hades' powers was granting the use of a helmet that made the wearer invisible. If such an object were available, I am sure Scorpio would be first in line to use it. Scorpio loves mystery and transformation—mystery in the sense that they don't like to reveal themselves to others and many spend their lives endlessly transforming their inner landscape. The focused energy of Scorpio must be expressed in creative activities. If their energy stays blocked within them then Scorpio can suffer from the "too much syndrome": too much feeling, too much food, too many relationships, too many drugs or liquor, or too much denial.

Scorpio is the only sign of the zodiac that has three symbols: the Scorpion, the Eagle, and the Phoenix. One type of Scorpio would rather sting himself to death than give up the pleasure of the sting. This is the Scorpion that can be caught in self-destructive patterns. The Eagle soars closer to the sun than any other bird and then controls his prey by swooping down on it, and the Phoenix rises again from his own ashes. Some unevolved Scorpios may linger on the darker side of life but ultimately all are moving toward transforming and re-creating themselves. This is the source of Scorpio's power. These descriptions sound very dramatic but Scorpio really is most comfortable dealing with the profound questions of life and death.

Scorpio is the third fixed sign of the zodiac after Taurus and Leo. The fixed signs are the steady powerhouses of the zodiac. All the fixed signs have a great deal of tenacity and strength. Scorpio's element is water. Unlike the seas and oceans ruled by Cancer and Pisces, Scorpio is represented by lakes and the water of marshes and swamps. I wouldn't recommend buying a bog for your Scorpio friend, but a fountain made with dark rocks or a terrarium could be a wonderful present. People born under the water signs are instinctual and feeling, but true to Scorpio's reputation they may keep their feelings hidden. Their feelings lie deep beneath the surface and they usually maintain a quiet, dignified exterior. Their very reserve can project a feeling of superiority and stubbornness in relation to others. Scorpios prefer to be in control, and like the other fixed signs, they hold opinions that can be inflexible. Sometimes humor is the best antidote to their intense personality. Scorpios usually have a wicked sense of humor and can use stinging sarcasm to make their points. If you have been stung by a Scorpio zinger, you won't soon forget it. You will also remember, however, the penetrating way your Scorpio friend or lover listens and how you almost always feel better after speaking with them. In love and friendship Scorpio is loyal.

Scorpios guard their privacy fiercely. More than any other sign they understand that knowledge is power. This makes them not only good detectives but usually secretive about themselves. Out-of-the-way places, such as a garage or basement, attract this sign and may be a place of retreat for Scorpio. I know one Scorpio who works for the phone company and *always* volunteers to try out new phone numbers. She has had so many phone numbers that very few people can keep track of her whereabouts, which is exactly how she likes it. There is a store in New York City that offers security and spy equipment for nonprofessionals. I have always wondered if the owner is a Scorpio.

Animals are usually drawn to the hypnotic energy of Scorpio. Many Scorpios feel more comfortable with the nonverbal communication possible with animals. They also enjoy being their pets' masters. One woman who had many Scorpio placements brought feral cats into her home and slowly domesticated them. She also had a great deal of success healing all her pets with unconventional remedies and herbs. Scorpios may dote on their pets and show them more outright affection than the people in their lives. The sign is usually not talkative. Scorpio rules snakes, spiders, and lizards. I know a therapist who wears a Spiderman T-shirt under her pants suit. She looks properly professional on the outside but also holds true to her Scorpio individuality on the inside. On hot days in the summer in New York I sometimes see "snake people." These are people who have snakes as pets and think nothing of draping them around their necks to take in the air. I have always wanted to ask if they are Scorpios but I am afraid of snakes and never got that close!

In terms of a home environment Scorpios usually like things simple and uncluttered. But if the Scorpios work at home, the home is overflowing with all the equipment necessary for them to delve into their work. I have also noticed that Scorpios like to decorate with objects that they use. For example, one woman had a black leather couch, her NordicTrack, and her son's Nautilus machine in her living room. That is what they used and all she needed. Scorpio rarely is concerned with what people think. Scorpio may be attracted to motorcycles or other machines that go fast. There can be a tendency in this sign of nudging fate. Scorpio should temper thrills with a cool head. If you have unlimited funds, give your Scorpio a Porsche or Lamborghini . . . but make sure they have completed a course in race car driving.

The above descriptions may seem a forbidding challenge when choosing a gift for your favorite Scorpio wife, friend, child, or husband, but you won't go wrong if you consider that the sign responds deeply to affection and never forgets a kindness or real consideration. Scorpio appreciates the effort a person makes almost as much as the gift itself. Natural psychologists, Scorpios discern the impulse or motivation behind a gift and it is this they often respond to. A Scorpio friend told me that his father asked his college friends what a good birthday gift would be. At the suggestion of his son's friends, the father gave his son, who was a composer, a collected set of the opera Wagner's *Ring Cycle*. In fact, my Scorpio friend meant that he wanted Tolkien's *The Lord of the Rings*. The most interesting part of the story was that my Scorpio friend appreciated his father's consideration so much that he really didn't mind that the present was not what he had in mind.

Colors and Flowers

Colors for Scorpio tend toward the darker tones: black, white, burgundy, navy blue, dark brown, and some gray and charcoal. Deep maroon is also a Scorpio color. The current fashion for black suits Scorpio and does not seem to drain their energies. I always recommend wearing red underwear, but alas, my advice is not always appreciated by Scorpios. Scorpio fashion is not busy or fussy. The men and women will not care if their clothes are out of fashion. If they are comfortable and look good, that's enough. One Scorpio friend wears a black jogging suit to all informal occasions. I don't believe I have ever seen her legs exposed, as she also wears dark stockings for work. This is part of her mystery.

Scorpio rules flowers and plants that thrive in marshy areas or lowlands. There are not many of these in the florist's shop; take a trip to the woodlands. Walking is the best exercise for Scorpio. If you are choosing flower arrangements avoid complicated ones. Scorpio ladies may be more content with long-stemmed red roses or calla lilies. White geraniums and poppies are Scorpio flowers. The heather that is found on the heath is also Scorpio-ruled.

Metals, Gems, and Materials

Before the discovery of Pluto in 1930, Scorpio was associated with the planet Mars and was thought to have a special affinity for the metals iron and steel. Now Pluto rules the sign and the metal for Scorpio is plutonium. I don't imagine there is any call for gifts fashioned from plutonium but Scorpio might appreciate the thought. Mars is still considered a co-ruler and all metals that are forged resonate with the sign. Iron decorative items such as the wrought-iron balconies of Scorpio-ruled New Orleans are a good example of metalwork that Scorpio would enjoy.

Gems that are bloodred, such as garnets or rubies, resonate with Scorpio. Usually Scorpio is attracted to jasper, jet, hematite, and dark agates. When choosing a stone or crystal the most important thing is to see what twinkles at you. In addition to the reddish stones, Scorpio enjoys smoky quartz crystal. The beautiful green stone malachite has also traditionally been associated with Scorpio. Carrying this stone may be cooling to Scorpio's intensity. Small, carved malachite animals are perfect decorative gifts for a Scorpio's home.

Astrologically speaking, there is not a particular material associated with Scorpio. In keeping with their love of darker colors, I would suggest black leather. Scorpio also enjoys dark worsted woolens and well-tailored suits.

Food, Herbs, Tastes, and Scents

Scorpios enjoy exotic food. Their preference may be predominantly for bitter tastes rather than sweet. Caviar, oysters, and red wine may be particular favorites. One Scorpio couple I know goes to a different ethnic restaurant every month. It is a safe and interesting way of seeing the world. Herbs that promote healthy digestion and elimination are beneficial for Scorpio. Senna tea may be particularly good. Other herbs and spices that Scorpio enjoys are specialty mustards, quinine, and hops, a major ingredient in beer.

The sense of smell is linked with the reproductive system and Scorpio will enjoy gifts that stimulate any and all hormones. Patchouli, musk, and heavier scents are all alluring to Scorpio. The perfume Passion comes to mind easily. The reproductive organs are the parts of the body associated with Scorpio; as you can imagine, this means *sex*. Scorpio is known as the sign of sex and almost all Scorpios are pleased with this association. Anything that confirms their fascination with power is appreciated. Sexy underwear, negligees, bathrobes in crimson silk, or even black sheets may be an appropriate gift for Scorpio. One client gave her Scorpio husband a set of black boxer shorts with HOME OF THE WHOPPER stenciled on the boxers. He loved it and loved her double for giving him the gift. When and if a Scorpio is experiencing low libido there is usually some energy block within the whole system. This may not be the type of information someone has while thinking about a gift for Scorpio, but if the subject comes up consider giving your Scorpio a gift certificate for energy work, or a balancing therapy, such as Reiki. Even a book on the subject could help Scorpio.

Travel

Unfocused travel may not be Scorpio's favorite activity. Scorpio likes to know exactly what is going to happen and to be in control of a situation. The many variables of travel can challenge their equilibrium. Scorpio-ruled destinations include Russia, Algeria, Morocco, and Norway. The beautiful, intricate tiles on homes and mosques in Morocco may be very interesting to Scorpio. An excellent gift for your Scorpio would be a wilderness trip. Consider the Grand Canyon or some other natural wonders. Scorpio enjoys the feeling of grandeur and awe that being in the wild can bring. Another consideration would be gifts to help secure and hide valuables during travel. Secret compartments in a purse or bag or luggage with very good locks suit Scorpio.

Sports

Physical exercise is important to keep all those juices flowing. Water sports and martial arts seem to attract Scorpios. These people are very in tune with the connection between the mind and body. Studying some form of meditation is a good way of channeling this sign's prodigious energy. Scorpio is comfortable around lakes and at the beach; however, they prefer shade and rarely expose themselves to the sun. Sports that attract Scorpio could be any of the martial arts, especially kickboxing or kendo. For regular hacking around, baseball, football, basketball, and running would probably be of more interest than tennis or golf. A Scorpio is a solitary person and enjoys long-distance or endurance sports. I would be curious to see if many marathon runners are Scorpio. In a list compiled by various sports experts of the fifty greatest North American athletes of the last hundred years, there were no athletes with a Scorpio sun and only one with a Scorpio moon. That was Chris Evert, the tennis player.

Intellectual and Artistic Interests

Spiritual study is of great interest to Scorpios. The sign usually has healing ability and is fascinated by the power of the mind. The penetrating ability of Scorpio's mind can get to the bottom of any subject they study. We see many great psychiatrists and doctors with Scorpio prominent in their charts. A number of this intense sign turn their powers toward religion and philosophy. Although sex is a ruling passion, there are people of this sign who choose to be celibate as a spiritual practice. Martin Luther, founder of the Reformation, and St. Augustine, the major leader of early Christianity, are two examples. Augustine was the profligate pagan who said, "Lord, make me celibate but not now." When he converted to Christianity and decided to devote his life to God, he wrote volumes on the unpredictability of sexual feelings. Philosophically minded Scorpios may enjoy his book *The Confessions.*

As Scorpio is the sign of creativity, it is not surprising that Scorpios usually have many creative talents. Many Scorpios paint or draw. Your Scorpio friend may find it relaxing to copy great masterworks or to study drawing techniques. Magic and magicians are another area that Scorpios may find interesting. Magic tricks, murder mystery games, the video game Dungeons and Dragons are all creative activities for Scorpios of all ages. Many Scorpios are excellent chess players. A beautiful, solid chess set is a great gift idea. Scorpios also love humor books and jokes of questionable taste.

Romance

Scorpio in love is a passionate affair. These people are committed to romance and like to express their deepest feelings in an intimate relationship. You still may not feel that you have understood all the depths of this sign but it will be a fascinating journey to share their intensity. The sign usually concentrates on a single relationship and is basically monogamous. There can be a jealous streak in Scorpio. Both women and men can be possessive. Mutual tattoos or a gift of some piece of clothing that both people could wear would suit Scorpio's notion of romance. Scorpio is also very responsive to scent and would enjoy perfumes with sandalwood and patchouli.

Well-Known Scorpios

In addition to a long list of artists there are numerous Scorpios in science and medicine. The first open-heart surgeon, Christiaan Barnard, was a Scorpio. Two giants of science—Marie Curie and Jonas Salk, the creator of the vaccine that wiped out polio—were also Scorpios. Biographies of these figures would interest Scorpio's probing mind. Scorpio might also appreciate a history of science and medicine written for the layperson.

There are a number of painters and visual artists born under this sign; Scorpios like to create in privacy and silence. Classical artists include the Dutch artist Jan Vermeer. His use of pictorial light is awesome and a book of his paintings would be a beautiful present for your Scorpio. Moving into more recent times, the Impressionist painters Monet and Alfred Sisley were Scorpios. Monet's water lilies are fertile, lush, and languid; they suggest depths of passion that Scorpio enjoys. Monet's paintings are available in countless reproductions, coasters, and even jigsaw puzzles! The giant of twentieth-century art, Pablo Picasso, was a Scorpio. I have seen quite a few Scorpio homes and offices with Picasso prints or large coffee table books prominently displayed. The sheer output of this artist is daunting, and when you consider that he changed so many of our ideas about modern art, his contribution is enormous. It is interesting that so much of his inspiration came from primitive art and fertility symbols, which are both Scorpio areas of interest. Georgia O'Keeffe was also a Scorpio. You can feel in the sensual color of her flower paintings the passion for living she had. She died in her late nineties, had been married to the great photographer Alfred Stieglitz, and in her later years her companion was a much younger man. The great sculptor Auguste Rodin was a Scorpio. Take your Scorpio on a trip to tour all the Rodin sculptures. There are also a number of reproductions of Rodin's work. His sculpture *The Kiss* may be of particular interest.

In the field of literature, two novels are examples of Scorpio artistry: Dostoevski's *Crime and Punishment* or *Notes from the Underground*. These books weave the Scorpio themes of sin, corruption, sacrifice, and redemption with masterful storytelling. The poets Dylan Thomas, Sylvia Plath, Ezra Pound, and John Keats were Scorpios; these fascinating artists got under the skin of human experience. The black humor of Kurt Vonnegut is an example of another Scorpio trait. His book *Slaughterhouse Five* is beautifully written and bittersweet. Last, the playwright and actor Sam Shepard is a Scorpio. Videos of his films are available and there are many books of his plays.

Scorpio showbiz personalities abound. Scorpio intensity can leap off the screen. Claude Rains, who starred in the classic film *The Invisible Man*, was a Scorpio; he was born on the same date as actor Richard Burton. These two British performers had voices like black velvet and were wonderful actors. Contemporary Scorpio actors are Leonardo DiCaprio, and David Schwimmer of the television show *Friends*. Some of the funniest performers in show business are Scorpio. Monty Python's John Cleese is certainly one of them. Others include Henry Winkler, Art Carney (who made a great team with Pisces, Jackie Gleason), Jonathan Winters, John Candy, and Mike Nichols. Before Mike Nichols directed, he performed comedy with Elaine May. If you have the opportunity to buy some of their early videos take a look at them before you give them to your Scorpio friend. They are deeply funny. Scorpio ladies are also very funny; Whoopi Goldberg and Roseanne Barr to name two.

One of the highest-paid actresses today is Julia Roberts and she is certainly a Scorpio. Her life is as private as she can get it and she manages to radiate a sexuality and power on the screen that transcends the characters she plays. She is an old-fashioned movie star. Other extremely talented actresses are Academy Award winners Jodie Foster and Sally Field; Meg Ryan, and Winona Ryder also have the Scorpio mystique.

Scorpio: Response to Celebrations and Occasions

BIRTHDAY

Scorpio assumes that everyone will know this is the day they slipped into the world. They will never make a big fanfare about a birthday but will remember until death who remembers and who forgets. Part of the secrecy of the sign will be to insist that no one should make a big deal of birthdays. It would be rare to successfully plan a surprise party for a Scorpio. They will intuit your plans and play along with the surprise. You may never even know that they knew all along.

CHRISTMAS / HANUKAH

Scorpio usually feels good around the holiday time. The long dark nights are comforting to them because nesting suits them, and many Scorpios enjoy the cold weather. The sign is generous and not frivolous about giving and receiving. One family with many Scorpios gave each person a book called *The Secret Knowledge of the Universe*. It seemed like a fitting gift if only for the title.

ENGAGEMENT / MARRIAGE

When Scorpio embarks on a project like marriage, it is usually with a serious intent. A Scorpio man will put a lot of time into planning the moment to propose and it will be a private affair. A Scorpio woman will have a definite sense that a proposal is coming and will be very clear about her answer. Engagement parties for either sex should freely indulge in all games with innuendo. Usually the home style is conservative. The one exception to this is if the couple is interested in art. Scorpio can enjoy primitive art or abstract art. The major quality necessary is that the work is intense.

NEW BABY

Scorpio parents are possessive of this new and wonderful addition to their home. The best gift family and friends could give might be time for the parents to get used to their new child. If you are giving a gift to a Scorpio baby think of gifts that soothe, such as tapes of water or ocean sounds. Scorpio babies sleep deeply and will need some time adjusting to morning light or waking up after a nap.

NEW HOME

Bill Gates is a Scorpio. The home he has built on the water in Seattle perfectly reflects his powerful personality and interests. Everything in the house is computerized and yet the dominant feel of the place is a fortress on the water. A protected place is a key ingredient for Scorpio. I have noticed that Scorpios can also live very well in small places. Gifts should be in black, whites, and browns. Feng shui practitioners usually eschew dried flowers because they suggest life that is passed, but Scorpio understands the mysteries of the life cycle and frequently enjoys dried flower arrangements.

ANNIVERSARY

Celebrate at home or by going out but let the evening end in the bedroom, and I don't mean asleep! Both Scorpio men and women need to know their spouses want them. The current fashion for jungle prints seems to me to suit Scorpios. Tattoos are also frequently found on Scorpios. Maybe the ideal anniversary present would be a tattoo of your love's name or initials.

VALENTINE'S DAY

The deep red of Valentine's Day cards is a Scorpio color. This sign wants passion on the day for lovers rather than romance. Women may enjoy the unique "black rose." It is a beautiful flower and evokes the mystery of male-female relationships. Scorpio really isn't happy without mystery. For a male Scorpio a black leather carryall or an elegant black pullover would be an excellent gift.

MOTHER'S DAY

A Scorpio mom holds her little ones tightly and privately. She is fiercely protective and will enjoy any gifts her kids make or give. A surprise breakfast in bed may not be welcome. The early morning is usually personal time for Scorpio moms and permission to stay abed may be the best gift.

FATHER'S DAY

Scorpio fathers are very nurturing and usually funny. A great gift would be humor books, tickets to a comedy club, or to any comedy. If your Scorpio dad is involved with sports, the best way to spend Father's Day would be sharing whatever sport he enjoys. Also special dates with sons and daughters are a great way to celebrate Father's Day.

GRADUATION

Scorpio is very in tune with rites of passage. Even if the student knows what they will be doing after school or university, these people appreciate the idea of moving on to another stage of life. Choose presents that will last such as a commemorative paperweight or a piece of crystal with the school's emblem on it.

THANK-YOU PRESENT

Scorpio would appreciate an indulgent thank-you present. Chocolates, a time-saver present, or some small piece of decorative glass for the home would be appropriate. Don't bother with a note; Scorpio communicates feelings directly and doesn't much care about etiquette.

ANYTIME PRESENT

A secret scavenger hunt to find a hidden present would be a great gift for Scorpio. If you don't have the time for such an adventure, give a gift such as an amulet or mineral that Scorpio can keep as a touchstone. Scorpio won't usually show surprise if you give them a gift on the spur of the moment; he or she will assume that you have been thinking of them.

Scorpio Gift Suggestions

SCORPIO MAN

Thrifty Saturn

CD of Gregorian chants
A beer stein
Murder mysteries
Scarlet robe
Horehound candy
Bottle of ouzo or absinthe
Classic white oxford shirts
Gourmet pesto
Imported cigarettes
Ripley's *Believe It Or Not*

Luxurious Venus

A hot tub
Erotic art
Long black leather coat
Black onyx cuff links
Personal lie detector
Home-brewery kit
Mahogany library stand
Nautilus exercise equipment
Pool membership
Fine red wine
Scuba diving equipment

Bountiful Jupiter

A submarine
Personal fortress

Grove of cypress trees
Cadillac with tinted windows
Snakeskin luggage
A private island
Trip to Morocco
Pyramid-shaped house
A Harley Davidson
A home wall safe
Vintage red wines

SCORPIO WOMAN

Thrifty Saturn

Apothecary jars
Book of witchcraft spells
Mud packs
Lapsang souchong tea
Black towels
Hematite ring
A divining rod
Dark chocolate
Organic espresso coffee
Black silk panties
Patchouli massage oil
Caller ID

Luxurious Venus

Malachite jewelry
Stiletto boots
Red Depression glass
Feng shui consultant
Aroma candles
Trip to New Orleans

Flamenco lessons
Set of oil paints
Alexandrite jewelry
Ivory silk blouse
Black body-suit
Antique garnet ring
Designer business suit

Bountiful Jupiter

Black Lexus
Topaz jewelry
A Moroccan villa
Georgia O'Keeffe Painting
Snakeskin shoes and bag
Waterford crystal
Black mink coat
Own business
Black-and-white marble bathroom
An island

SCORPIO BOYS AND TEENS

Stealth bomber model
Inflatable Tyrannosaurus rex
Chemistry kit
Cryptography book
Teddy bear
Eagle T-shirt
Spiderman comics
Spiderman Toy
Lava
Lava rock
Book on the history of magic

Dungeons and Dragons game
Spy kit
Black T-shirts
Motorcycle jacket
A wet suit
Book on snakes
Tattoos
Navel ring
Pocket knife
Maroon sweater
Ultraviolet lamp
Tapes of classic horror films
A pet gecko

SCORPIO GIRLS AND TEENS

A diary with a lock and key
A treasure chest with a lock and key
Garnet ring
Magic tricks
Tattoos
Red silk bustier
Stuffed "Nessie," the Loch Ness monster
A magic wand
Turquoise jewelry
Books on Native Americans
White mice
Puzzles
Henna body art
Book by Emily Post
Synchronized swimming lessons
An ecosphere
Panties with red hearts

A burgundy robe
A black cat
Small dogs (Corgis, dachshunds)
Sandalwood incense
A Slinky
Leopard print clothes
Magenta comforter
Yin-Yang symbol

Sagittarius

November 22–December 21

SAGITTARIUS
A Mutable Yang Sign

SYMBOL:	The Archer
RULING PLANET:	Jupiter
ELEMENT:	Fire
BODY PART:	The hips, thighs, and liver
FAVORED POSSESSIONS:	Large furniture, goblets, a wheel of fortune
COMMUNICATION STYLE:	Expansive and enthusiastic
HOME STYLE:	Wide-open and rustic
COLORS AND METAL:	Rich purples and blues, platinum
FOOD, PLANTS, FLOWERS:	Mulberry, cinnamon, oak trees, carnations
PARTNERSHIP STYLE:	Good-natured and some-times fickle
RULING PASSION:	Honesty
PHILOSOPHY:	High-minded thoughts im-prove the world, and if they don't, have a good time.
GEMSTONES:	Topaz, sapphire
WISHES OR GOALS:	To live in a free, rambling world
UNCONSCIOUS DESIRE:	To find an all-encompassing philosophy
FOR GIFT-GIVING, KEEP IN MIND:	Sagittarius likes adven-tures more than things.

Character Traits and Symbols

Sagittarius is the zodiac's eternal optimist. His symbol is the centaur, who is half human and half horse. The centaur carries a bow and aims his arrows high into the world of ideas. Sagittarius is always ready to take a chance. He is the gambler of the zodiac and usually has good luck. Sagittarius roams through life seeking out the value of experience and pondering the meaning of life but does not waste time being too deep about the matter. The centaur gallops away and moves on. This sign's motto is "Don't Fence Me In." Sagittarius wants freedom to express his ideas and freedom to move around. In general, when considering presents for these amiable people, think big, free, unencumbered, and casual.

The sign is a mutable sign, meaning that it is changeable. Mutable signs occur in the last part of a season as the climate is moving toward the beginning of the next season. This changeability may be part of the Archer's charm and also his/her unpredictability.

There is no other sign of the zodiac that loves surprises more. One of the best gifts for a Sagittarius is to say, "Let's go on a surprise adventure." Or if your Sagittarius friend suggests a jaunt or expedition and you leap to your feet and say, "I'm ready." Half the fun for Sagittarius is going on the spur of the moment and leaving cares behind.

Jupiter, the chief Roman god, is Sagittarius' ruler. Jupiter (or Zeus, in Greek mythology) is the head of all the gods and throughout mythology has symbolized abundance and even excess. In astrology this planet is called the greater benefic, because its positive nature betokens blessings and bounty. Jupiter also rules size: all large objects, animals, and spaces. In terms of giving gifts to Sagittarius, avoid anything miniature. If you buy wineglasses make sure they are deep-bowled and hold a generous amount. A Sagittarius would rather have a big box of chocolates than a few dainty morsels. Moderation is a challenge to Sagittarius because if one is good, more is better. There can be weight problems if Sagittarius doesn't get enough exercise. Taking a long walk every day is the best way for Sagittarius to keep balanced mentally and physically. These people need to stretch their legs and absorb the sights and sounds around them. A small apartment or a confining desk job is a recipe for a very nervous and unhappy Sagittarian.

You may notice that your Sagittarian friends frequently are mopping up spilled milk or broken glass. The sign's exuberance extends to their physical space and they tend to gesticulate expansively while they talk. They are not clumsy, just so involved in self-expression and moving freely that anything blocking their way might take a tumble. Keep the dinner table free of extraneous things. A gift of large napkins might be a good idea. If you are considering gifts for a family with a number of Sagittarians, a lazy Susan for the table might be a welcome addition. The Archer's home space usually is open with uncluttered space. Beanbag chairs or a few free-form pieces of furniture would be welcome gifts.

Sagittarius is the sign of the ruling clergy, such as bishops, cardinals, and the Pope. Capricorn rules the day-to-day priests and religious vocations but Sagittarius is known for the splendid and colorful ritual of the Church, as well as providing spiritual guidance. More than a few of my Sagittarian friends enjoy having dark woods and furniture reminiscent of pews in their homes. You may also want to give a gift of chalice-shaped glasses or vases.

I must mention the famous Sagittarian bluntness, which may be called foot-in-mouth disease. Your Sagittarius friend, lover, or spouse finds it very difficult to hide his thoughts or feelings. Tact is not an attribute of this sign. They never maliciously try to hurt someone's feelings but their communication is straightforward and they pride themselves on their honesty and candor. Usually their speech is good-humored and they won't mind a bit if you tell them they are full of beans or should consider learning diplomacy. Sagittarius for the most part will not believe that they have said anything tactless, but they will happily say, "You have a right to your opinion." They are usually very talkative, so you will have ample opportunity to observe how ingenuous their words can be. One use of Sagittarian candor is the sign's excellent ability to motivate and inspire people to work together. For business associates or friends, consider giving books on the philosophy of winning or how to improve optimism and team spirit. *The Seven Habits of Highly Successful People* by Stephen R. Covey or Dale Carnegie's *How to Win Friends and Influence People* are some examples. Anything that helps fuel Sagittarius' vision of maximizing a group's potential and creating cheerful working conditions is a bull's-eye gift.

Sagittarius sees the humor in everything. Contrary to expectations, people in this sign may not be good joke tellers because they start laughing midway through the story and blow the punch line. Their laughter, however, is infectious and they enjoy humor books, as well as cartoons. One particularly cold Easter a Sagittarian friend arrived at dinner with a bonnet decorated with Christmas balls and wore it throughout the entire dinner. Pranks and mischief are diversions that Sagittarius loves. Sagittarian kids will howl at whoopee cushions, fake snakes, etc. A surprise visit to a joke shop could be a memorable gift for Sagittarius.

Colors and Flowers

Like the other two fire signs, Aries and Leo, Sag enjoys vibrant colors. Unlike Aries and Leo, whose palette tends toward reds and oranges, Sagittarius enjoys rich blues, greens, and purples. I always think of the Ghost of Christmas Past in Dickens' *A Christmas Carol*, a jolly fellow, with wreaths of mistletoe in his hair, quaffing wassail and wearing a rich blue cloak trimmed with ermine. This exuberant image suggests all that is best about Sagittarius. Flowers that resonate with Sagittarius are carnations, gladiolas, and poinsettias. If you want to send flowers to a Sagittarian, choose large arrangements or a big bunch of flowers rather than one delicate blossom. Large urn-shaped vases are both decorative and useful items that Sagittarius would enjoy. Sagittarius also has an affinity with oak trees. At the ancient site of Dodona in Greece, Zeus' (Jupiter's) oak was the site of an oracle that predated the Delphic Oracle. A flower arrangement that includes oak leaves and perhaps acorns would resonate with your Sagittarius.

Metals, Gems, and Materials

Sagittarius has traditionally been associated with all woolen material and men's clothing. Many members of this sign wear clothes well and are partial to dramatic yet casual styles. I have noticed that Sagittarian women like suede shirts and coats. All valuable furs, such as mink, ermine, and sable, are Sagittarian materials. As Sagittarians are often tall and well-proportioned, fur coats or cloaks are becoming styles for them. Other materials to keep in mind for gifts are velvets and brushed velours. Richly colored velvet dresses or smoking jackets would be wonderful gifts for Sagittarians.

The metals platinum and tin are Jupiter-ruled. For gifts of jewelry, choose platinum or you may hear a few comments from your candid Sagittarian. Tin has been used recently in many interesting home furnishings. Brushed tin in particular makes a very handsome mirror frame.

Jewelry and gems interest Sagittarius for their

beauty but they do not usually like to be responsible for wearing expensive stones. The gems Sagittarius enjoys are deep blue sapphires, amethyst, and some raw turquoise.

Foods, Herbs, Tastes, and Scents

All warm spices and scents, such as clove, cinnamon, and cardamom, are Jupiter-related. If you think of the warmth and richness of mulled wine on a cold winter day, you have a feeling for tastes and scents that appeal to Sagittarius. Making a clove orange is a holiday ritual that any Sagittarius, young or old, would enjoy. Wild game, pheasant, and quail are meats that appeal to Sagittarius. There are many specialty shops that ship these delicacies at holiday times. Another great food gift for Sagittarius would be roast chestnuts or marrons glacés. Sagittarius rarely likes bland food. I had a Sagittarius uncle who was miserable when the doctor prohibited dill pickles and horseradish. As soon as he could resume his spicy diet, it was as if a cloud had lifted.

The herbs that suit Sagittarius are those that improve digestion and circulation. Jupiter rules the liver and any natural therapy that detoxifies the liver would be productive for Sagittarius. Sometimes all that exuberance takes a toll on the body. Borage, liverwort, and bitter chocolate are all good possibilities.

Travel

Sagittarius loves travel and is not fussy about the arrangements or the accommodations. If they feel the urge to go, then they will manage with first class or coach. The important thing is the voyage itself. Gifts of portable luggage and travel items that are light and convenient will always be appreciated. There is an entire catalogue devoted to practical and elegant travel clothes and useful things to take along for trips. You may find your Sagittarian reading it to stimulate his imagination. Sagittarian countries are Spain, Hungary, and Dalmatia on the northern coast of Yugoslavia. One interesting city that Sagittarius rules is Avignon, France. During the fourteenth century, due to political infighting, the Papacy was relocated to Avignon. The beautiful Palace of the Popes remains today. As Sagittarius is the sign of bishops and the Pope, it would be interesting for this philosophically minded Sagittarius to visit Avignon. Other interesting Sagittarian cities are Cologne, Germany, and Naples, Italy.

Sports

Sagittarius is an outdoor sign and whether they are on a trip or moving around their neighborhood, Sagittarians love to be on the move. Hiking boots, jackets with tons of pockets that allow the arms to swing freely, or polar fleece vests are all good ideas for gifts. One Sagittarius friend zoomed around New York City on his bike, which he called his horse, wearing a green parka and a camouflage vest with many pockets. All means of motion appeal to Sagittarius. Consider skateboards, scooters, in-line skates, skis, and even a red wagon. The areas of the body ruled by Sagittarius are the hips, thighs, and legs. Those who do not get enough exercise could find they have problems with their legs or sciatica. It is very important to stretch enough before working out or running. Leg warmers, insulated jogging pants, and good sneakers are good gift ideas and important to keep Sagittarius healthy and injury-free. If you live with a Sagittarius, you may have to remind them to take it easy as the sign usually "does first and thinks later." Sagittarians excel at team sports, such as basketball and baseball. They are usually very coordinated and also enjoy tennis, golf and horseback riding. Polo is a sport tailor-made for Sagittarius. If you give gifts of sports equipment make sure it is lightweight and requires minimal maintenance. To encourage Sagittarius to relax after their workouts, give them gifts such as Tiger Balm, quince bath salts, sage bath essence, or an almond oil massage.

Some of the best athletes have Sagittarius prominently placed in their charts. In a list of the top fifty athletes of the last hundred years, the second most represented sign was Sagittarius. Reggie White, Joe DiMaggio, and Ty Cobb were all Sagittarians. Outside of baseball, Martina Navratilova, Arnold Palmer, Mark Spitz, and Oscar Robertson all had Sagittarian moons. Many of these sports figures also devoted themselves to philanthropic causes after they retired.

Intellectual and Artistic Interests

In the same way that Sagittarians need physical motion to keep their bodies in balance, they need to contemplate big and important ideas to keep the brain and heart balanced. Books on philosophy or about great thinkers are usually very good gift choices for Sagittarians. Most Sagittarians are religious but few are dogmatic. Religions are interesting because they consider questions such as "Why are we here?" "Where are we going?" and "What is the best way to live?" Your Sagittarius friend may feel close to a particular saint and never go to church. Toward the middle years of a Sagittarian's life, he or she may become very interested in spiritual practices. It is as if all the traveling and motion of their younger years transforms into an inward journey. A trip to a retreat center, yoga lessons, or t'ai chi study might be very welcome. Many Sagittarian parents I know take their children to different religious ceremonies every week. This smorgasbord approach serves two Sagittarian values: spiritual exploration and travel. Gifts that are reminiscent of religious objects usually please Sagittarius. Tibetan table chimes, chalice shapes, the Egyptian ankh symbol, or a cross are all good choices.

Artistically, there are many Sagittarians in the performing arts. The theater is a natural outlet for their expansive nature and good humor. All the fire signs have the ability to inspire people and Sagittarian directors are especially effective. In the visual arts Sagittarius may be partial to painting large canvases or creating pieces of sculpture. Gifts of acting lessons, backstage theater tours or tickets to a musical would also be appreciated.

Romance

Sag and romance is a vast topic because there are usually so many opportunities for Sag to flirt. The sign is strongly attracted to the opposite sex and is eager to meet as many of them as possible. There is not much sentiment in Sagittarians and they rarely nurse a broken heart. What really wounds their feelings is any lack of honesty or sneakiness. These people are very principled and want to be recognized for it. Tokens of friendship such as a poem that expresses your feelings or a book by a writer you both enjoy are excellent ways to please a Sagittarius lover. The sign has little concern for conventional attitudes toward love and marriage. Marriage may be a tough commitment for many Sagittarians but if they give their word, they will keep it. Popular books on love and romance are not a good idea for these people because they delight in finding their own solutions to finding a guy or girl. Following the standard rules of courtship is too simple and predictable for them. Sagittarius wants freedom to discover a person their own way.

Well-Known Sagittarians

Many well-known Sagittarians are leaders and politicians. In addition to these people's considerable leadership abilities, they each have a larger than life personality. Sagittarian Winston Churchill was known for his huge appetite and ability to consume the better part of a whiskey bottle a day. He never appeared to work hard and conducted much of the business of state from his bed. Ed Koch's cheerful question "How am I doing?" engaged New Yorkers and kept him a popular presence in the city even after his mayoral term ended. Other Sagittarian leaders are Charles de Gaulle and Jacques Chirac. Each of these leaders boosted their constituents' spirit in addition to maintaining the government. Biographies of any of them would be interesting gifts.

Performers Marisa Tomei, Bette Midler, Ellen Burstyn and Goldie Hawn are all Sagittarians. They are striking women and very individual performers. Bette Midler started her singing career with a blunt and risqué cabaret act and then developed her film career with a wide variety of roles. Ellen Burstyn started her career doing television comedy, then won an Academy Award for *Alice Doesn't Live Here Anymore*. In her middle years she became very interested in spiritual healing and performed one of her most memorable roles in *Resurrection*. Her character was paralyzed in her legs and hip (both Sagittarius-ruled) and cured her own illness. She then went on to heal other people. If you haven't seen the movie, take a look and definitely consider giving a copy of the video to your Sagittarian friends. Last, in addition to Goldie Hawn's wonderful acting and very funny movies, she makes an annual pilgrimage to India for spiritual renewal. Sagittarius always aims his/her arrows high!

Male Sagittarius performers and film artists are Brad Pitt, Boris Karloff, Sammy Davis Jr., Dick Van Dyke, and Noël Coward. Noël Coward was an extremely witty man who used his Sagittarian bluntness to humorous effect on many occasions. When planning to cross the Atlantic, he said, "I'll go on an Italian liner where there is none of this women and children first nonsense." Recordings or filmographies of any of these artists would keep Sagittarius happy for hours. I have also noticed that many male Sagittarians have an encyclopedic knowledge of film history and Hollywood lore. Let me not forget two outstanding Sagittarians in film: Harpo Marx and Steven Spielberg. Both artists have a childlike innocence and joy that they translate into their work. Spielberg's interest in creating large-scale projects with universal themes has defined an entire genre of film. His Sagittarian love of size extends to his large family and the number of humanitarian foundations that he has created.

In literary fields three of the world's major poets were Sagittarians: Emily Dickinson, Rainer Maria Rilke, and William Blake. Blake's poetry and woodcuts define for me the exuberance and high ideals of the Archer. Purchase his books *Songs of Innocence* and *Songs of Experience*, and you will give a present of great beauty and meaning. One of Blake's well-known aphorisms is: "If you be in a passion some good you may do, but no good if a passion be in you." I think his line sums up spiritual insight native to Sagittarians.

For Sagittarian music lovers consider the symphonies of Beethoven. The elegant and passionate opera singer Maria Callas was a Sagittarian. There are many biographies about her dramatic life and opera lovers prize her recordings. Another exuberant musician was Hector Berlioz. His *Symphonie Fantastique* is a beautiful work. For popular music lovers, examine works by Paul Simon, Sinead O'Connor and Jermaine

Jackson. Paul Simon has traveled throughout the world for musical inspiration. The current superstar Britney Spears is a Sagittarius. There are numerous vidoes and CDs of each of these artists.

Sagittarius: Response to Celebrations and Occasions

BIRTHDAY

Since Sagittarius is usually the life of the party, a birthday will be a fine occasion to celebrate the joy of life. Sagittarius is usually not shy about his/her age and will enjoy humorous cards about decrepitude. Sagittarius always has the last laugh because they remain young at heart eternally. A theme party might be a welcome present. Childhood games such as a relay race could be just the adventure at a birthday outing for Sagittarians of any age.

CHRISTMAS/HANUKAH

This is a great time of year for Sagittarius. The winter solstice comes after their birth month and they love to keep warm in winter with the celebrations of the holidays. Velvet is a favorite fabric for these people. Perhaps a velvet opera cloak or fur hat is the perfect dramatic touch. Sagittarius is also mindful of the religious meaning of the holidays and usually gives generously to good causes, such as their church or temple.

ENGAGEMENT/MARRIAGE

Courtship, engagement, and marriage are likely to be whirlwind events for Sagittarius. Choose nontraditional presents. A collapsible pup tent might be a perfect gift. That way Sagittarius could take his home with him. When popping the question to a Sagittarius woman, it's okay to make it casual as long as it is sincere and the environment is interesting. Under a waterfall strikes me as a perfect place. The ladies don't require romantic trappings and will probably know when marriage is in the air. Think about an emerald and diamond engagement ring. The marriage itself will probably be lavish and highly individual with lots of fun and activities. An outdoor site is ideal. The best present might be registry at a travel agency.

NEW BABY

A Sagittarius parent delights in the unfolding curiosity of a child and will look forward to raising a bright, honest individual. Gifts of snugglies, car seats, or anything that aids easy motion for parents and child will be most welcome as well as gifts that encourage mental or physical exploration, such as a mobile or a scooter seat. Sagittarius babies love company and being around people. Give durable toys, as the babies are usually quite strong and love to throw things around.

NEW HOME

Avoid small tchotchkes. Jupiter-ruled people like large definite objects in their homes. Many Sagittarians enjoy large paintings of landscapes. Serving platters also suit their sense of abundance. Pottery in blues and greens or faience is preferable to porcelain. I've also noticed that Sagittarians like beanbag furniture. The casual style and possibilities of many shapes appeal to their free-form nature.

ANNIVERSARY

An adventure away from home is the best idea. Both men and women love new experiences. If you can't go far away, think of something unique, like walking across the Brooklyn Bridge or hiking through the hills to a restaurant. Perhaps one balloon for each year you have been married would make your Sagittarian spouse grin with delight?

VALENTINE'S DAY

Ardor is second nature to Sagittarius but the sign doesn't like to feel compelled to express himself/ herself just because there is a holiday. A Sagittarius might whisk you away to a casino or an amusement park rather than give what's typical. Another Sagittarian way of celebrating the holiday would be to find a *huge* box of chocolates and invite a half dozen people to share it; after all, for a Sagittarius in love, the more the merrier.

MOTHER'S DAY

Sagittarius mothers are breezy and not brimming over with gooey maternal emotions. They enjoy their children and do not try to control them. A good present on Mother's Day would be to visit a zoo or the gift of beginning archery lessons. Minimize home activities and maximize adventure.

FATHER'S DAY

Sagittarius fathers consider the most important part of parenting to be teaching their children about moral values, in particular: honesty. They also value cultural education. This will usually be accomplished with slight impatience but good humor. On Dad's day, do something sporty, funny, or cultural. I remember one Sagittarius father who beamed with pleasure when he overheard his kids saying, "No, it was Van Gogh who cut off his ear, not Monet." This conversation was after a Father's Day outing to the museum.

GRADUATION

Sagittarians greet the future with characteristic optimism and curiosity. Graduations represent an opening to many new interesting possibilities. Sagittarians may not have a clear idea of what kind of work they want to do. If you encourage their ideals you will be surprised at what they come up with. There is a book by Paulo Coehlo called *The Alchemist*, which seems to me a perfect gift for a Sagittarius' graduation. It is a fable that describes a young man searching for his fortune and all the experiences and difficulties he encounters as he pursues his dream. Read the book before you give it to your Sagittarius. It is quite inspiring.

THANK-YOU PRESENT

Don't stand on ceremony with Sagittarius. A hearty thank-you is just fine, and if you forget, that's okay too. If you want to give a present, think of something humorous or fun. A toy like a Yo-Yo might be a novel idea. For business associates a large cornucopia or basket of fruit would be just the thing.

ANYTIME PRESENT

Giving a gift just for the fun of it will please any Sagittarian in your life. Whatever your sign is you may also expect to get "anytime gifts" from your Sagittarius friend. Choose a special jar of honey or a comfortable T-shirt with I'M LUCKY written on it. Sagittarius doesn't mind sharing his good nature with the world. Of course, taking a plane, train, or drive is always a good anytime present.

Sagittarius Gift Suggestions

SAGITTARIUS MAN

Thrifty Saturn

Roast chestnuts
English Leather aftershave
Bedside prayer book
Amethyst geode
Jogging clothes
Trip to the racetrack
Blue wool socks
Case of Cracker Jacks
Travel books
Framed diplomas
An incense burner

Luxurious Venus

Archery set
Passport case
Fitness pedometer
Royal blue cashmere sweater
Fur hat
Set of classical literature
Personal treadmill or NordicTrack
A tuxedo
Trip to a dude ranch
Graduate education
Vicuna sports jacket

Bountiful Jupiter

A stable full of horses
Handmade leather saddle
A racetrack
Chinese altar table
Big-game safari
A trip around the world
Large Oriental rugs with center medallion
An Irish wolfhound
Set of leather bound classical literature
A home with fireplaces in every room
A villa in Italy

SAGITTARIUS WOMAN

Thrifty Saturn

No jet lag homeopathic remedy
A green wallet
Red roses
Eucalyptus honey
Bottle of anisette
A treasure chest
Leg warmers
Green tea
Apricot-colored scarf
A cloved orange

Luxurious Venus

Purple velvet comforter
Blue topaz jewelry
Alpaca coat
Carbuncle ring

Graduate education
Trip to Spain
Copy of Da Vinci's equine prints
Fringed suede skirt
Olive green silk blouse
A large family-size incense burner

Bountiful Jupiter

A prize racehorse
Sable coat
A trip to Singapore
Church pew furniture
A statue of Jupiter
A ranch
Golden retrievers
Topaz jewelry
Cases of Madeira sherry
A loft
A home with plenty of open space

SAGITTARIUS BOYS AND TEENS

Hobby horse
Totem pole
A pup tent
Wool ski cap
A stuffed reindeer
Four-leaf clover
Acre of land
Book on religions of the world
Rollerblades
Skateboard
Racing bike

Blue velvet comforter
Green velour shirt
Science magazine
Leather pants
A St. Bernard puppy
Stuffed toy elephant
Sugarcane
Tin horn
A wallet
Book on whales
Framed diplomas
Dice
A fishing pole
Good running sneakers

SAGITTARIUS GIRLS AND TEENS

A stuffed toy horse
A rocking horse
Amethyst ring
Mini trampoline
A rabbit's foot
Multicolored T-shirts
A fur hat
Peacock feather earrings
Jasmine soap
A Raggedy Ann doll
A Wrinkle in Time by Madeleine L'Engle
A pony
Strawberry print clothes
Large green purse
Topaz ring
Blue velvet jumper

Stuffed whale
Gymnastic lessons
A Native American dream catcher
A cowboy hat
Trip to a horse-breeding farm
CDs by Sinead O'Connor
Travel tote
Basenji dog
Hip hugger pants
Ballet tights and leotards

Capricorn

December 22–January 19

CAPRICORN
A Cardinal Yin Sign

SYMBOL:	The goat
RULING PLANET:	Saturn
ELEMENT:	Earth
BODY PART:	The knees and skeletal system
FAVORED POSSESSIONS:	A briefcase, fine art, pewter ware, fine wool clothes
COMMUNICATION STYLE:	Serious
HOME STYLE:	Classic and conservative
COLORS AND METAL:	Brown, black, ivory, dark green, lead
FOOD, PLANTS, FLOWERS:	Meat, beets, ivy, pine cones, elm trees
PARTNERSHIP STYLE:	Committed and concerned with practical comforts
RULING PASSION:	Desire to reach the goal
PHILOSOPHY:	Slow and steady wins the race
GEMSTONES:	Turquoise, amethyst
WISHES OR GOALS:	To live with a clear hierarchy
UNCONSCIOUS DESIRE:	To throw caution to the wind
FOR GIFT-GIVING, **KEEP IN MIND:**	Capricorn likes classy, important gifts

Character Traits and Symbols

Capricorn's symbol is the goat climbing up the mountain. Climbing up rocky crags, where there is sparse food and perilous heights, Capricorn pursues any goal with great determination and concentration. This sign considers life serious business and is very interested in success, whatever that may mean to them. Sometimes the success that comes to them is not material but spiritual. Capricorn often works in nonprofit organizations or is involved with a cause. Their most significant personality trait is the fervor they have for their endeavors and causes. Their strong power instinct, drive, patience, and work ethic sustain them while they are climbing toward their goals. Accompanying Capricorn on their journey through life is a very dry wit and sense of humor that pokes fun at themselves as well as at all human foibles. Capricorn is reliable, responsible, and very pragmatic.

Capricorn is the last cardinal sign of the zodiac.

The cardinal sign of Aries (fire) begins the astrological year and the cardinal sign of Capricorn (earth) ends it. Metaphorically, it is interesting to see that the leadership sparks that Aries initiates can only be realized in the world by the practical and structural leadership of Capricorn. Slowly and steadily Capricorn will always get where he or she wants to go.

Saturn is Capricorn's ruling planet. In ancient times Saturn (the Greek Chronos) was the planet farthest from the sun that could be seen with the naked eye. Saturn rules time, challenges and limitations in life, and old age. He was not considered a cheery god but everyone respected the force of his wisdom and patience. Indeed, in mythology when Saturn fled from Mount Olympus to Italy, his rule initiated a Golden Age, a time when people lived in perfect harmony. The feast of the Saturnalia was held every year during the winter. During this time no war could be declared, slaves and masters ate at the same table, and people gave one another gifts. It sounds a lot like Christmas. Many holidays, in fact, have their origins in the progression of the astrological signs. The winter solstice on December twenty-first inaugurates the sign of Capricorn and represents a powerful point in the cycle of the seasons as it heralds the return of the sun's light. Christianity celebrates Christmas at this time, which announces the birth of Christ as the coming of the light to the world. In mythology and ancient custom there are many correspondences with all the major religions and astrological signs.

Saturn in astrology is called a malefic planet because its influence delays or hinders expression. We don't usually like the effects of Saturn because we are forced to think concretely, to plan, and to consider all the real world ramifications of our actions. One French lady in heavily accented English told me, "Saturn make me down." I always say, "Yes, and without Saturn, life would have no structure and no limits." We all need the reality check Saturn offers. Even Sagittarius must structure his enthusiasm or he would be a joyous nincompoop! Look closely at your Capricorn friend or spouse and watch the methodical way he or she plans anything. It is a lesson in patience and diligence.

Choosing gifts for this sign offers many opportunities because Capricorn, an earth sign, feels at home in the physical world. The air and fire signs enjoy material things but are more at home in experiences and ideas. For water signs the most important part of life is feeling. The earth signs—Taurus, Virgo, and Capricorn—believe that we are on the earth to manage the concrete and tangible world. Earth signs are very sense oriented and delight in manifesting their thoughts and feelings in the material world. A Gemini might love to spend all day talking about a great idea to help the children of the world. A Capricorn will be busy planning how much a foundation would cost, who they could call to help develop the idea, and how to incorporate the whole idea and make it tax deductible.

At home, Capricorn loves to display photos of their immediate family as well as ancestors as far back as they can be traced. Saturn, as I said before, rules time. Thoughtful gifts would always be photo albums, scrapbooks, or picture frames for the growing family collection. One friend gave her Capricorn mother restored photos of her grandparents. It was a big hit. Both Capricorn and Cancer (the opposite sign) enjoy genealogy. Books on how to research your family tree or genealogy charts would be gifts that start Capricorn off on a subject near and dear. A Capricorn client was very interested in grave rubbings and traveled to all the cemeteries where her ancestors were buried and made rubbings of the gravestones. Giving these as gifts to the rest of her family was a big success.

Saturn also rules the passage of time and Capricorn is more comfortable with aging than many other signs. There is something comforting for them about knowing the events that have passed and feeling the richness of experience. Capricorns are usually long-lived and remain sturdy and active throughout their lives. One of Saturn's symbols is an old man with a scythe harvesting time; it is reminiscent of the Father Time figure we see around the New Year. All time-pieces, clocks, and watches belong to Capricorn. Many Capricorns collect clocks. Gifts of an antique watch or a brand-new Swatch would be great for conscientious Capricorn.

As I mentioned before, Capricorn rules big business. The corporate structure is familiar to Capricorn because they think in terms of hierarchy. Progress is measured in terms of the stages they must pass through to achieve their goals. A Capricorn's office should be well-decorated. Gifts such as blotters, desk sets, a leather briefcase, or even a well-functioning pencil sharpener make Capricorn feel efficient and powerful. If you imagine the elegance of a country club or a private library, you will have a good picture of the kind of atmosphere Capricorn likes.

Colors and Flowers

Colors that Capricorn enjoys are the browns (especially chocolate brown), beige, winter white, and black. Dark evergreen and maroon are also favorites. Capricorn rules big business and government, as well as priests and nuns. Don't look for cassocks or habits as a basic style for Capricorn personalities but you may notice that they enjoy wearing a basic understated, elegant uniform. Capricorn stands out with their style because it usually is just right for them. They are not ostentatious but mindful of the impression they give.

Gardening and working with flowers is a wonderful hobby for Capricorn. They have green thumbs and love to mix decorative rocks and statuary amidst the flowers. Flowers and plants for Capricorn are white foxglove, purple rock cress, pansies, all mosses, holly, ivy, and cypress, willow, and yew trees. Lawn statues, even a garden gnome faintly resembling one of the Seven Dwarfs, may hit Capricorn's funny bone. As much as Capricorn enjoys prestige, odd homey touches please their sense of continuity and history. When giving cut flowers to a Capricorn, choose flamboyant, colorful blossoms. One Capricorn I know had birds of paradise and ginger flowers sent from Hawaii to her during the gray winter months. Her home was decorated in the muted shades typical of Capricorn and the tropical flowers provided much-needed color.

Metals, Gems, and Materials

It might not be surprising that Saturn rules all minerals (including gems) and rocks. That means that all precious and semiprecious stones are excellent gifts for Capricorn. Jet, hematite, white onyx, and garnets have a rich color that accords with Capricorn's nature. Capricorn likes to be around minerals. Large geodes, quartz crystals, and just plain old rocks make Capricorn feel secure. One client was forced to travel a great deal for business and didn't much like it. He told me he always picked up a rock from wherever he went and kept it with him. When he returned home he placed it in his garden. With the current vogue for fountains, I have seen a number of fountains that would delight a Capricorn. A fountain flowing over smooth black pebbles or a granite-based fountain would add water to Capricorn's earth.

Capricorn will prefer classical jewelry settings and white gold, silver, or platinum to yellow gold.

Capricorn may also enjoy creating garden paths with slate slabs and marble statuary. Mosaic tile is frequently found in Capricorn homes. A kit to make your own mosaics or furniture with mosaic tiles would be a wonderful gift. I know one Capricorn woman who created a mosaic in her bathroom with shards of dishes and smooth glass. The bathroom was entirely white tile and then there were glints of wonderful colors and different textures from the mosaics—very artistic and practical. She found a use for a lot of mismatched dishes.

Ceramic pottery interests Capricorn; consider giving dishes with an earthen glaze. Many Capricorns build their own homes or make extensive renovations. A marble-topped table or tile or granite counters would be a wonderful contribution to Capricorn's dream house. Also consider ceramic trivets or hot plates.

All leather is Capricorn-ruled. Frequently both men and women have very good bone structure and can wear leather suits or pants with great panache.

Foods, Herbs, Tastes, and Scents

Capricorn may have a great fondness for sour foods such as dill pickles, preserved lemons, and sour cream. In general, they are meat-eaters and enjoy rich stews and hearty winter fare. Barley is a grain traditionally associated with Saturn and although mushrooms are ruled by Cancer, their opposite sign, a nice bowl of mushroom barley soup would be a perfect meal on a cold winter's day. I have also noticed that Capricorn enjoys salty foods such as caviar and anchovies. An interesting food taste for a Cap is quince. There are many Middle Eastern recipes that use quince for flavoring.

Pine scents and bath oils are excellent gifts for Capricorn. Taking baths is in general a soothing activity for this very determined earth sign. The skin is considered under Capricorn's rule. Both men and women have beautiful complexions. Normally sedate Capricorn ladies sometimes squeal with delight when presented with special cream for dry skin on the elbows. Men and women favor smoky scents such as sandalwood or cedar. Facial masks, emollients, bath oils, and a good rubdown with rosemary-scented massage oil are enjoyable gifts for both men and women.

Travel

Capricorn is not overfond of traveling. They are very clear that the effort of packing, flying, etc., has to be for a good reason. The most interesting location ruled by Capricorn is India. This is hardly a casual trip but may be worth the time and effort. The spiritual orientation of India is something most Capricorns understand intuitively. Closer to home, Boston is Capricorn-ruled. The reputation for white-gloved propriety does seem very Capricornian to me. Boston, however, was also the home of the Tea Party, which contributed to the beginning of the Revolutionary War. As I mentioned before, Capricorn can be a fierce fighter for equality and people's rights. It is interesting that both Boston and India have "Brahmins," indicating a social hierarchy or caste system. Other Capricorn destinations are Mexico and Lithuania. Cities that have been linked with Capricorn are Oxford, England; Constance, Switzerland; and Brussels, Belgium. Brussels has been a central city in the development of the European Economic Community and well fits Capricorn's qualities of organization and thrift.

Sports

Capricorn rules the knees, elbows, teeth, and all bones. Our bones form the body's structure and Capricorn is the sign that rules structures of all kinds.

When we feel the limitations of Saturn, it is important to remember that, without limits and the "bones" of any project, our efforts are amorphous. On a more practical level, Capricorns must protect their elbows, joints, and knees. Frequently, people in this sign run for exercise. Running is solitary and Capricorns usually appreciate the time to think. It is a good sport but at the first sign of knee problems, visit the chiropractor or osteopath or change your sneakers. Gifts for Capricorn athletes include a stopwatch, warm-up suits, a massage gift certificate, and a set of weights. Capricorn enjoys weightlifting, since it requires a combination of concentration and discipline. Plus, since Capricorns love all forms of measurement, they will be happy to notice their increasing ability to lift ever heavier weights. Most people in this sign are slender and are not likely to bulk up too much from weight training.

Another sport Capricorn usually enjoys is golf. Tiger Woods is a Capricorn. I think the concentration needed for putting and long-distance calculations for drives suits Saturn's sense of discipline. Well-known sports figures include the great champ Muhammad Ali and the ball player Sandy Koufax. Joe Louis, another great fighter, had a Capricorn moon, as did Jim Thorpe and Willie Mays.

Romance

In romance, Capricorn is discreet and measured in his or her passions. Your Capricorn lover may never say they'd really like silk undies or boxers with red hearts, but if you gave such a present you might see them flush with delight at receiving such a "frivolous" gift. Consider gifts for your Capricorn lover that are the exact opposite of their self-image and you will make him or her feel cherished and happy. Capricorns are very loyal and do not move in and out of relationships easily. As with fine wine, love ages well for Capricorns and the enigma of the sign is that just when you think you have figured them out they do something surprising. The way to melt your determined Cap's heart is to find a soft, luxurious gift that they would never consider buying for themselves. A cashmere wool sweater or vicuna jacket might be the perfect thing to warm Capricorn's bones.

Intellectual and Artistic Interests

Artistically Capricorns are slow to express themselves. As children they may have been given the feeling that drawing or singing wasn't important enough and squelched their native abilities. The good news is that it is never too late to start exploring creativity. One Capricorn client who was sixty-four told me that she felt pink inside but only managed to express gray outside. She started painting and made the most colorful, fanciful drawings you can imagine. If you want to encourage a Capricorn to express themselves artistically consider buying a hobby kit for mosaic making, or creating tile-topped furniture. A course in sculpture would be a revelation for them. Even modeling clay would be a good idea.

Ideas are of interest to Capricorn in terms of their

practical application. People in this sign can be rigorous in examining the ramifications of ideas and questioning their beliefs. Ultimately they may decide that many ideas must be taken on faith and cannot be reasoned out. An excellent gift for Capricorn is an historical time line atlas. Seeing when and how ideas have influenced events throughout history would interest these diligent people.

Well-Known Capricorns

The number of well-known Capricorn artists gives us a wealth of gift-giving possibilities. First, the great painters Matisse and Cézanne were Capricorns. There are many beautiful reproductions of their paintings available, quite a few coffee table books, and even coasters, paper napkins, and place mats with some of their more famous paintings.

In keeping with the sign's rulership over faith and teaching, Capricorn boasts some of the greatest spiritual teachers, scientists, and humanitarians. Books about any of these people or a collection of their writings would resonate with Capricorns. Louis Pasteur and Stephen Hawking are both Capricorns. These two men explored science in ways that profoundly altered the world. Stephen Hawking's book *A Brief History of Time* is an in-depth study of Capricorn's favorite subject and symbol: time. Two other great Capricorn humanitarians were Dr. Martin Luther King and Dr. Albert Schweitzer.

In philosophical matters Alan Watts, one of the first Westerners to write about Zen practices, was a Capricorn. Maharishi Yogi, the spiritual teacher for the Beatles, and the creator of the Transcendental Meditation movement, was born January 12. Gurdjieff, a spiritual teacher in the beginning at the twentieth century, wrote a book called *Meetings with Remarkable Men*. The book was also made into a beautiful film and is available on video. Interestingly, the philosophy and spiritual practice he taught was called simply "the work." That has always struck me as a particularly Capricorn way of looking at spiritual development. Last, Carlos Casteneda was born on Christmas Day. His books about his Mexican spiritual teacher and the Yaqui way of knowledge influenced many people in the sixties and seventies.

Some of the most elegant and striking female Capricorns are in show business. Faye Dunaway, Diane Keaton, and Cate Blanchett are all beautiful women and fascinating actresses. When Faye Dunaway accepted her Academy Award for *Network*, she said, "I didn't expect this so soon." What a Capricorn gal! She knew where she was headed. It was just a matter of time. Diane Keaton has always interested me because like many Capricorns she is very cool on the outside but gives the impression of great passion inside.

Two very elegant actors are Cary Grant and Anthony Hopkins. Cary Grant defined sophisticated comedy. He aged gracefully and remained true to his abilities. Biographies of any of these performers or copies of their movies are great gifts. Kevin Costner, Mel Gibson, and Jim Carrey are also Capricorns.

Lest you feel Capricorn is humorless or gloomy, consider that one of the greatest and funniest performers of all time was Ethel Merman. She was famous for her no-nonsense approach to singing and acting. Her standard line was, "I know my lines. What have I got to worry about?" Her biography is worth reading because she was such a larger-than-life character. The King of Rock 'n' Roll, Elvis Presley, was a Capricorn. In addition to his fame as a singer he created a business empire. His home, Graceland, still attracts thousands of visitors. There are countless Elvis souvenirs that your Capricorn friend might get a kick out of. If your Capricorn friend is feeling melancholy, a good dose of Elvis' "All Shook Up" or "Burning Love" is just the prescription. Other noteworthy popular singers are David Bowie, the rapper LL Cool J, Patti Smith, and heartthrob Ricky Martin.

Capricorn: Response to Celebrations and Occasions

BIRTHDAY

Capricorns are comfortable with birthdays because to them, older means better. Unless he/she has settled into rigidity, life improves with the accumulation of years. Make sure your celebration is orderly for children and that the birthday boy or girl can sit at the head of the table. Come to think of it, adult Capricorns also want to be at the head of the table, presiding over their birthday and surrounded by family and friends. The best presents include soft and luxurious items that Capricorn secretly wants but won't buy for himself/herself. Gifts that denote status are also a good choice.

CHRISTMAS/HANUKAH

This is Capricorn's time of the year. Some may feel put out because they must share their birthday with general holiday-making but the winter solstice, the advent of Capricorn, marks the beginning of longer days as the sun begins its motion north once again. Capricorns can feel the energy increasing minute by minute. Emphasize traditional family gatherings and some kind of social service during this time. Abundant evergreens and pine scents are all enjoyable for Capricorns.

ENGAGEMENT/MARRIAGE

Merging a life with another person is serious business for Capricorn men and women. They do not make a commitment lightly and are keenly aware of the financial ramifications of their decision. A Capricorn man will plan the time he wants to propose, will see to all the details, and be fairly certain that the woman in question will accept. The wedding is likely to be very tasteful, traditional, and calm. Capricorns like the idea of a china and silver registry. One double Capricorn couple received five crystal wine decanters for their wedding. They kept them all and started a collection.

New Baby

Capricorns tend to decorate in monochromatic color schemes. With the arrival of a new baby, decorating the home with yellows, pale blues and some tapes of ocean sounds would benefit both the parents and the new baby. Capricorn parents are welcoming another person into the family firm. They will relish books on enriched education and will appreciate gifts of children's books they remember having read as children. Also, books that help a Capricorn parent establish a routine for their child will be most welcome. The babies would enjoy a lot of bright colored toys and need a lot of physical affection.

New Home

The home is likely to be comfortable without ostentation. Don't shock Capricorn with a bright showy set of Fiesta ware or wild print tablecloths. Good quality home furnishings, an up-to-date barbecue or houseplants are all good ideas for a housewarming. Remember, if you find any interesting geodes or minerals, Capricorns might love to display them in their home.

ANNIVERSARY

To Capricorn, once he or she is married, romance is the steady commitment of living together. To celebrate this commitment, take a Capricorn woman out to a classy restaurant or buy the new rug you have been talking about. Celebration for Capricorns can be either a luxury treat or something practical. Both presents testify to the family unit that a married Capricorn treasures. On the other hand, a Capricorn man will appreciate a gift that supports his lighter side. One couple I know goes to a water theme park on their anniversary. It's a great way to indulge in silliness.

VALENTINE'S DAY

Capricorn men might want to keep a book of love poetry in their drawer and pull it out on this sentimental holiday. A few tender words from this normally quiet sign will do much to keep the love fires burning. Cards, chocolate, roses, and a nice dinner are all fine ideas but a Capricorn woman will most appreciate feeling the security that she is loved and hearing about it. For your Capricorn male Valentine, consider playing hooky and walking in the woods.

MOTHER'S DAY

Motherhood is a role that responsible Capricorns do well. They may be strict but they won't shirk the job. To celebrate, give Mom a spa day or the gift of take-out meals for a week. Taking a family photo every Mother's Day could be a tradition that she will look forward to. Capricorn mothers derive pleasure from watching their children mature and enjoy sharing educational or cultural activities with their older children.

FATHER'S DAY

Capricorn is the sign that symbolizes a person's relation to the rules of society. It values the role of the father as the head of the family and teacher of children. Dad will feel honored if you take him out to a restaurant and show him he has raised polite, well-bred children. Gifts of aftershave, leather accessories, a good book, or a pipe would be appreciated.

GRADUATION

There is usually a clear path for Capricorn upon finishing any level of school. They know where they want to go and will be very responsible about searching for jobs and making a living. A photo album with pictures spanning their student days would be a great gift. Cash isn't a bad idea either. Capricorn will not feel slighted that you couldn't decide on a gift.

THANK-YOU PRESENT

Capricorn likes to be thanked in a quiet and discreet manner. Sending flowers, a card, or homemade cookies are all suitable ways to thank a Capricorn. Thank-you notes are not as essential as they are for a Libra but a note keeps you in Capricorn's network. If there is no reciprocation for kindness, Capricorn will move on to a more fruitful relationship.

ANYTIME PRESENT

The look of appreciation and perhaps amazement on a Capricorn's face when receiving an unexpected present or courtesy may encourage friends and relatives to surprise them more often. Capricorn does not demand attention but quietly glows when he/she gets it. Give a gift such as stacking boxes or a flower arrangement, or take over a chore that your Capricorn usually does. The gift doesn't have to be flashy. The fact that someone made the effort counts the most.

Capricorn Gift Suggestions

CAPRICORN MAN

Thrifty Saturn

Weather forecasting station
A Farmer's Almanac
Granite paperweight
Family photo album
Heavy socks for boots
Dark brown sweater vest
A miner's lamp
Dark lager beer
Garden tools
Visit to a cave
Homemade sauerkraut
Leather key chain
Visit to a climbing wall

Luxurious Venus

Vintage bomber jacket
Leather document case
Winter white cashmere sweater
Antique wristwatch
Old coins
Ebony furniture
Hiking boots
Leather boots
A fossil collection
A bearskin rug
Calculator in a leather case
Book on architecture

Leather-bound first edition

Bountiful Jupiter

A farm
Heated garage
A mountain retreat
A marble bathtub
Inlaid table
A vintage VW
A skeleton clock
A slate patio
A chauffeur
A waterfall
Closet of tailored suits
A big truck
Treasury bonds
Rare manuscript

CAPRICORN WOMAN

Thrifty Saturn

Black bear paper towel holder
A carriage clock
Mosaic trivet
Wooden candle holders
Dry red wine
Currants
Patchouli soap
Gardenia plant
Rosemary bath oil
Aged balsamic vinegar
Poetry by Edgar Allan Poe
Hematite beads

Collection of leather belts

Luxurious Venus

Brown leather pants
Pewter dishes
Victorian jet jewelry
Onyx picture frames
Ivory silk blouse
Wooden hourglass
Russian tea glass holders
Terra-cotta planters
Faience china
Charcoal colored towels
A garden angel sculpture
Engraved napkin rings

Bountiful Jupiter

Teak patio furniture with umbrella
A Volvo
Forest of pine trees
Star sapphire ring
Handmade clothes
A pyramid-shaped home
Ceramic fountain
Vacation in a five star hotel
Domestic servants
A grandfather clock
A mantel clock

CAPRICORN BOYS AND TEENS

Time-telling Yo-Yo
Galileo's thermometer

A puppet theater
A stuffed koala bear
A toboggan
Black T-shirts
Gray sweater
Tape on how to relax
Camel ride
Sage green shirt
A stuffed toy donkey
Ice cream maker
A junk trunk
A gargoyle
An old-fashioned gas mask
Books on rock collecting
Mountaineering equipment
Charcoal and sketchpad
Sour ball candy
Trilobite fossils
A scarecrow doll
Play-Doh
Snow shoes
A play tunnel
A toy tractor

CAPRICORN GIRLS AND TEENS

Tooth fairy box
Bear slippers
Stuffed toy panda bear
Puppets
Removable tattoos
Make-your-own-tile kit
Modeling clay

Underground hideout
A stuffed toy raccoon
Brown leather skirt
Turquoise bracelet
A burgundy chenille shirt
Leather mittens
Pumice stone
A cocker spaniel
Hematite ring
Pine bath essence
Green leather wallet
A cuckoo clock
Black velvet skirt
A scarecrow
Set of dominoes
J. D. Salinger's *Catcher in the Rye*
Movies with Mel Gibson
Topaz ring

Aquarius
January 20–February 18

AQUARIUS
A Fixed Yang Sign

SYMBOL:	The Water Bearer
RULING PLANET:	Uranus
ELEMENT:	Air
BODY PART:	Ankles and circulatory system
FAVORED POSSESSIONS:	Lamps, electronic gizmos, unusual hats
COMMUNICATION STYLE:	Erratic and eccentric
HOME STYLE:	Eclectic and airy
COLORS AND METAL:	Electric blue, violet, aluminum
FOOD, PLANTS, FLOWERS:	Kiwi fruit, kumquat, elderberry, birds of paradise
PARTNERSHIP STYLE:	Unconventional and cool
RULING PASSION:	Desire to live a unique life
PHILOSOPHY:	Individuals and friendship make the world go round
GEMSTONES:	Aquamarine, lapis lazuli
WISHES OR GOALS:	To create a brotherhood of all people
UNCONSCIOUS DESIRE:	To dictate how people should relate to each other
FOR GIFT-GIVING, KEEP IN MIND:	Aquarius will like anything that is unique and unusual.

Character Traits and Symbols

Aquarius, the sign of invention, individuality, group consciousness and genius can have two distinct character types because originally the sign had dual rulership. Before the discovery of Uranus in 1781, Aquarius was ruled by Saturn and was more closely identified with the cautious and conservative nature of Saturn—somewhat like Capricorn. Ancient astrologers had predicted a planet, which they called Ouranos, and which in mythology was the sky god. With the electrifying discovery of the planet Uranus, astronomers verified what ancient astrologers had predicted. Astrologers then observed that many people born under the sign of Aquarius had characteristics that belonged to this new planet. Today, as we are moving into the Age of Aquarius, we see some Aquarians who harken back to Saturnine influences, but many are those who move forward into the unknown, unpredictable excitement of Uranus.

Aquarius is the sign of the inventive, rugged individualist who remains mindful of the needs of society and humanitarian goals. The Aquarian will enjoy gifts that appeal to both their individuality and their consciousness of the group. For example, a certificate designating a portion of the rain forest preserved in your Aquarian's name would be a personally and socially meaningful gift. However, don't expect these people to be flighty because their vision carries them far into the future. Aquarius is a fixed sign. It is located in the middle of the winter season and all fixed signs (Taurus, Leo, and Scorpio) are powers to reckon with. Aquarius might tell you to do something for the good of humanity but he or she wants it done in any case. There have been more Aquarian presidents of the U.S. than any other sign. And these presidents have all been very influential ones: Abraham Lincoln, Franklin Delano Roosevelt, and Ronald Reagan are the most significant.

Aquarius is an air sign. This sometimes confuses people, as the sign's symbol is of a water bearer pouring water from a large vase. Ancient sources record that, when the constellation of Aquarius rose in the Middle East, it corresponded with a period of floods and rain; hence the symbol may pertain to a weather pattern in the ancient world. The symbol, however, is also metaphorically correct if you consider that Aquarius' greatest joy is to pour forth knowledge or ideas for all humanity. The Internet (Aquarius-ruled) is a perfect example of individual ingenuity in service of the collective. The Internet is also egalitarian, a cherished value of Aquarius. Books on surfing the Web, learning how to use new technology, computer games, screen-savers, or doodads to perch on your computer are all things that Aquarius enjoys.

Aquarius rules electricity. Many people in this sign have a knack for tinkering with electronic equipment. They may be musicians with synthesizers or electric guitars. They will rarely have trouble setting up their computers, VCRs, DVDs or installing a self-dimming lighting system. I have noticed frequently that Aquarians enjoy unique lamps or sources of lighting in their homes. One Aquarius loved to show off his lamp that lit up when you touched it. It was a favorite moment for his kids, and guests always enjoyed it, too.

Being an air sign, Aquarius also enjoys all communication technologies and ideas, and the more unique the better. Telephones, cell phones, antique Morse code machines, or the latest e-mail Palm Pilot is the right gift for Aquarians. Don't worry about getting a sentimental gift. Aquarius is more interested in how something will help them move into the future. The sign rarely wallows in the past and can change affections, relationships, or jobs very abruptly. If, however, they are stuck, like the other fixed signs Taurus and Scorpio, they can remain in their pattern longer than other more flexible signs.

At home Aquarius likes lots of natural light and usually prefers houses on a hill or apartments in a high rise. There is always something slightly eccentric about the decor in an Aquarian's home. One woman I know decorated a corner of her apartment with a circular mattress covered with purple silk and feather boas. This "retreat corner" was blocked off from the rest of the space by a bookcase and faced the window in her high-rise apartment so she could sit and dream.

This sign also loves well-designed technology. Airplanes, air travel, even spaceships are all ruled by Uranus. A ride in a personal jet or helicopter would probably thrill most Aquarians. When we get to the point of traveling through space, I am sure Aquarius will fill up the passenger lists.

Colors and Flowers

Aquarian colors are electric blue, violet, mauve, turquoise, and all streaked mixtures of color like Joseph's coat. The color scheme for Aquarians encompasses the entire rainbow. Rainbows are, in fact, an Aquarian image. If we use all the colors of the rainbow we can express different parts of our personality. For example, a young woman who had six planets in Aquarius came to me and she was *stuck*. Nothing was changing in her life. She wore all black and sunglasses indoors. "First," I said, "the black has to go; consider periwinkle." She looked at me as if I were recommending a fashion disaster. However, a few months later she told me that a friend had given her a periwinkle pashmina shawl! She wore it constantly and it seemed to lighten her life. She initiated some artistic projects of her own and began to "unstick" herself.

In general Aquarians are not keen on house plants. They like flowers that have interesting shapes like Thai orchids or coxcombs and may be partial to silk flowers. Any new breed of flower or crossbred tree would be interesting to Aquarius. Choose flowers that are white or the color of blue hydrangeas. Many Aquarians prefer to stay indoors and keep their minds busy. Being in nature is not a physical need as it is for Taurus and other signs.

Metals, Gems, and Materials

There are many jewelry designers who have Aquarius emphasized in their charts. The gems aquamarine, black pearls, and sapphires all suit Aquarius. Jewelry in a very modern design as if it were a piece of sculpture is very Aquarian. I have seen jewelry made of wire and gems almost like the model of an atom and when I inquired about the designer I found she was an Aquarius. Other gems associated with Uranus are lapis lazuli, chalcedony, jasper and amber. The color of lapis seems particularly appropriate for this sign. This beautiful blue stone has been used for sculpture as well as jewelry.

The metals associated with the sign are uranium and radium . . . not, obviously, good for personal wear. White gold, platinum, or silver would be preferable to Aquarius. There is a mineral called rainbow titanium that will interest Aquarians. It is a striated mineral with shiny metallic colors. Give a small stone to your Aquarian so he can toss it from hand to hand. It might help with Uranian restlessness.

All fabric with an iridescent sheen or fabric with metallic thread is pleasing to Aquarius. Aquarians also favor distinct hats. I think it might help them to keep their heads warm while they are inventing new thoughts. Giving a purple or electric blue hat with a festoon of metallic ribbon could cement a friendship with an Aquarian.

Food, Herbs, Tastes, and Scents

True to their unique nature, Aquarius enjoys eclectic food. These people usually have strong constitutions and can eat almost anything. They may go through various food fads because they read an interesting theory about eating a certain kind of food. Popcorn seems to be a popular food for Aquarius. One client makes up a big batch to snack on and seasons it with curry. It is her own invention!

Physical restlessness is a characteristic of Aquarians. Some seem to have too much electrical energy in their bodies and must fidget or move constantly. They may have trouble sleeping or feel their brains are zooming with too many thoughts. Calming herbs are chamomile and valerian. The sign rules the body's circulatory pathway and the nervous system, and the calves and ankles. Keeping an even flow of energy is a challenge for Aquarius. Give your ready-to-experiment Aquarian a session at the acupuncturist. It would be a great introduction to a therapy that will keep his or her body in top form.

Scents that are astringent such as cucumber or witch hazel are pleasing to Aquarius. For perfume choose scents that are light and not overly sweet. Myrrh, bitter orange, and elemi are some that come to mind.

Travel

Since a trip to the moon is not yet possible, Aquarius will have to make do with planet Earth. Spur-of-the-moment trips and abrupt changes of plans are the hallmarks of Aquarian travel. These people can enjoy sleeping on a cot or in a luxury hotel. Many prefer traveling to the mountains, where the air is clear and cold. The plethora of handy travel gadgets available, especially when they aid communication, are definitely gifts that Aquarius would enjoy. Destinations that might resonate particularly with Aquarians are Sweden, Lithuania, Poland, and Russia. Interestingly, Warsaw, Poland, has some of the most artistic and colorful neon signs (both Aquarian-ruled) in the world. A wonderful trip for Aquarius would be to Mozart's home in Salzburg, Austria.

Sports

In keeping with Aquarius' rulership of the circulatory system, the best exercise is one that keeps the blood and energy moving steadily throughout the body. For Aquarians who might not be interested in contact sports, yoga or a martial art that includes the mind and body is the best exercise. Mindless aerobics or working out for Aquarius can create more nervous tension. Dance, low-impact aerobics, or t'ai chi are all good ideas. Aquarians also excel in both team sports and individual competition.

Aquarius is the most represented sign in a list of the top fifty athletes of the last hundred years—all sports from basketball to boxing. This list includes

Michael Jordan, Wayne Gretsky, Jack Nicklaus, Hank Aaron, and Jackie Robinson. The Olympic diver Greg Louganis is an Aquarius. Louganis once said that his major talent was understanding the "rhythm of the day" and devising his workouts accordingly. His statement is an inciteful comment on the mind and body connection. Babe Ruth, one of the greatest baseball players of all time, was an Aquarius. Give your Aquarian a Walkman with a rhythmic tape to play while exercising. It will keep them amused and centered. A supply of colored T-shirts would also be a great gift. Aquarius likes gifts that are useful.

Intellectual and Artistic Interests

Aquarius is a spiritual seeker because they see so clearly that society needs a belief system to function at its best. You may find your Aquarian pursuing a New Age religion or participating in a traditional church or temple, but they will think through all the teachings for themselves. Astrology is a very Uranian endeavor. Books on extraterrestrial life, theories about the beginnings of the universe, science fiction, or ancient mythology are topics that stimulate Aquarius' imagination. Giving a gift of a miniature planetarium to project a picture of the starry sky on your bedroom walls would be a wonderful gift.

Aquarius is the sign of genius and you never know how these people will manifest their creative energies. Aquarians usually have writing and musical talent. However Aquarius creates, they will probably work best with an erratic schedule. Conformity is not their strong suit. Visually, they are able to see new uses for old things. An Aquarian I know makes mobiles from old keys. The different size keys create an interesting visual effect and the sounds as they move in the breeze make a beautiful melody. Also with the growth of software programs for design many Aquarians can start to develop their artistic skills. Most people of this sign seem to have a knack with computers and programming.

Romance

Romance and Aquarius is sometimes an uncomfortable fit. Both men and women are very interested in friendship and companionship but are neither gushy nor very concerned with the world of watery feelings. The pleasure in intimate relationships is exchanging ideas and building something together for the future. The most reliable indication that the Aquarian is "in love" may be that they act as if they do not like you. Everyone is an Aquarian's friend, and if he or she is smitten, then factor X is at work and they rather resent the exclusivity that being part of a couple implies. However, Aquarius is very keen on principles and if they make a commitment they will keep it. The most important thing to consider with Aquarians and relationships is that they need freedom to do their own thing. They are unpredictable. One friend told me her Aquarian husband, a sociology professor, was on vacation solo, taking a bus trip from New York to Florida, then through Louisiana and Mississippi. In my mind buses are the transportation of last resort but she said, "Different strokes for different folks." They had a great marriage because neither got in the other's way. Surprise your Aquarius lover with an offbeat present, such as their name in a neon sign, that confirms his or her individuality and you will keep the steady fires of your relationship burning. Aquarius loves surprises almost as much as Sagittarius does.

Well-Known Aquarians

There are more Aquarians than any other sign in the Hall of Fame. The preeminent Aquarian artist was Mozart. His music is sublime. He began composing while still a child and performed for the crowned heads of Europe. His life has been the subject of two Broadway productions, a film, and countless biographies. Now psychologists have studied his music and concluded that listening can increase babies' intelligence. *The Mozart Effect* is a book that describes these experiments. Mozart recordings, his biography, or his sweet letters to his family as he toured Europe are wonderful and stimulating presents.

The first musician to adapt classical music to the guitar was Andrés Segovia. He pioneered transcribing Bach's music for the guitar and initiated a new direction for guitar music. One of the three great tenors of our time, Placido Domingo, is Aquarius. In addition to his incredible voice, he has worked for organizations that aid underprivileged children. In contemporary music, flamboyant Alice Cooper is Aquarian. A particular favorite of mine is the jazz musician Stan Getz. His song "The Girl from Ipanema" typifies a cool sexiness that I associate with Aquarius. In rap music the big daddy of all rappers,

Dr. Dre, is Aquarius, as is Snoop Dogg, his protégé. And Justin Timberlake of *NSYNC is also Aquarius. I am sure as technology and music develop we will see other Aquarian artists inventing unique musical instruments as well as new musical styles. Gifts of CDs or a collection of song lyrics would be excellent gifts.

Writers abound under this sign. Charles Dickens was Aquarius. His stories and novels entertained but were socially conscious as they unmasked the horrendous working conditions in nineteenth-century London. Curling up on a winter's day with a copy of *Bleak House* or *Little Dorritt* would be a peaceful way for Aquarius to relax. There have also been countless film and musical adaptations of Dickens' work. The poet Lord Byron was Aquarian and again we see the combination of social concerns and artistic interests. In addition to his poetry he died fighting for liberty for the Greeks because it suited his notion of preserving classical history. More contemporary writers are James Joyce and Virginia Woolf. James Joyce revolutionized literature in the early twentieth century by emphasizing the sounds of words in addition to telling a story. Virginia Woolf also experimented with literary forms and her essay *A Room of One's Own* is an early work advocating the view that women need independence for their artistic abilities to blossom. Books by these authors all would be interesting to Aquarians. And if your Aquarian's genius means that he or she hates to read, many of these authors' works have been translated into film and video.

In film and show business it is interesting that two of the pioneer filmmakers D. W. Griffith and Sergei

Eisenstein were Aquarian. Their masterpieces *Birth of a Nation* and *The Battleship Potemkin* were films that concerned the social and revolutionary interests of the day. Aquarians typically fight for causes that are right and just and can benefit the largest number of people. A fine example is Paul Newman. He is an actor, a humanitarian, and a philanthropist. His interest in auto racing illustrates one of the daredevil traits that Aquarius can be foolhardy with. Newman, however, trained for racing and safely managed a second career in the sport. One of the most versatile actors of the last fifty years was Jack Lemmon. He did comedy and drama and won an Academy Award for *Save the Tiger*. The film was a scathing indictment of American materialism and amorality. It is truly worth seeing. Other Aquarian performers are Alan Alda and Gene Hackman. John Travolta is an Aquarian and an avid pilot. He flies his own jet and considers flying one of his greatest joys. As I mentioned before, Aquarius rules all air travel.

Aquarian actresses are individual and eccentric. Vanessa Redgrave is probably one of the greatest actresses in the world. She is also involved with many political causes and her work for the Palestinians has created personal difficulties for her, but she has not given up her cause. Another example of Aquarian individuality is Mia Farrow, who has adopted many children, some with disabilities. Both these ladies have used their fame to benefit a larger group of people. Their biographies are interesting reading and following their idiosyncratic careers is fascinating. Jennifer Aniston of *Friends* is an Aquarian. She and her husband, Brad Pitt (Sagittarius), have a good blend of fire and air in their charts. Currently Ellen DeGeneres is a well-known Aquarian who sparked controversy as the first openly gay woman on prime time. Again, Aquarius is an explorer and breaker of conventions.

Probably the best-known Aquarian person in show business today is actress, talk show host, publisher, writer, and humanitarian Oprah Winfrey. This woman has created an industry out of spreading knowledge. Her book club publicizes books that she feels create positive images for people. Her magazine is a collection of interesting articles on personality and how to develop happiness and her show has defined the talk show milieu for years. She was nominated for an Academy Award for *The Color Purple*. She came from a poor background and has made a significant contribution to society. Her great success is based on popularizing big ideas and making them accessible to many different kinds of people.

Aquarius: Response to Celebrations and Occasions

BIRTHDAY

Aquarians like their birthdays because they mark progress into the future. A group activity or party is a good idea but Aquarius would also be content solo or with a few friends. It all depends on how much activity there is in their lives at the time. A surprise party would not be hard to organize because Aquarians always have tons of friends. The only hard part would be making sure the guest of honor gets there. He or she may find some interesting experience along the way and be too involved to make the party. Best presents would be friendship knots, a parakeet, or a neon sculpture.

CHRISTMAS / HANUKAH

Traditions and routine are not friendly to Aquarius. They may say, "Tradition is for people who don't have anything else better to do." However, the feelings of generosity and good will that the holiday season brings is a value Aquarius holds. Breaking traditions when it comes to holiday celebrations will keep your Aquarian interested. How about a blue Christmas tree? Aquarius would love it.

ENGAGEMENT / MARRIAGE

A man asking an Aquarian woman to marry him will already be in love with her iconoclastic nature. The idea of marriage may come as a pleasant surprise to her, so pop the question unexpectedly and she will likely say yes. Consider a beautiful aquamarine or an entwined engagement and wedding ring. She won't mind if you shop together for something just right. The wedding of an Aquarian could run the gamut from a large party to a small gathering on top of a mountain. Square china plates or crystal glasses with squiggly stems could provide that unique touch as gifts to the Aquarian bride or groom.

NEW BABY

A fascinating addition to the home! Aquarian parents will be intrigued and amazed at the uniqueness and unpredictability of their new baby. Aquarians usually have erratic schedules anyway so a new baby won't seem disrupting. Best presents are toys that develop the child's potential. Remember, *The Mozart Effect*. The Aquarian baby will love to be around groups of people and will usually not startle easily. Surprises are intriguing even to little ones.

ANNIVERSARY

Consider something new and different to celebrate your holiday. A ride in a helicopter or hot air balloon might be just the adventure to plan for your Aquarian sweetie. Don't get stuck in a rut and don't expect sentimentality from your Uranian spouse. Redoing all the windows in the house could be a super gift.

VALENTINE'S DAY

It is interesting that the day that celebrates lovers is within the sign of Aquarius. This is the sign of brotherly love and friendship. With all their friends, Aquarians will send more valentines than any other sign. For his or her particular love, flowers and chocolates will probably not be the first choice. A more enjoyable gift would be a disco ball or a night out dancing. It is possible that Aquarius is so busy zooming around or thinking about his or her latest theory or idea that they forget entirely that it is Valentine's Day!

MOTHER'S DAY

Uranian mothers are good pals to their children. But they don't thrive on sentiment and can be detached. Usually on their holiday they want a change of pace. Maybe the kids could give her dessert first thing in the morning or a gift certificate to a health club for a good workout, then soaking in the Jacuzzi and taking a sauna. Be inventive and the Aquarius mother will feel that she has raised perfect children.

FATHER'S DAY

An Aquarian dad considers his children the vanguard of the future. He may take them to tough neighborhoods so they can see how other people live but also may sit and go over their science lessons with them. Avoid at all costs giving him the standard tie, slippers, or wallet as gifts on Father's Day. An Aquarian dad wants surprising gifts and might love a vintage radio or some nifty electronic gizmo.

GRADUATION

An Aquarius' plans after school aren't likely to be clear or thought out. These people could travel for a while, then get a job, then travel, then write a successful novel, and then travel for a while. A good gift idea would be a phone calling card so they can keep in touch with home wherever they are.

THANK-YOU PRESENT

Manners for the sake of politesse don't cut it with Aquarius. If you aren't sincere, don't bother. Aquarius can give people they don't care to associate with the breeze faster than any other sign. On the other hand, if they do want you in their circle, you can thank them with a call, an e-mail, a multicolored bunch of flowers, or find a skywriter to write your thanks in the clear blue sky.

ANYTIME PRESENT

You may be walking down the street and see an eccentric hat in the window or an electronic gadget and think of your Aquarian friend or spouse. Give in to the impulse and you will make someone very happy. The story of how you happened upon an object and how it prompted you to think of them will be worth as much as the gift itself.

Aquarius Gift Suggestions

AQUARIUS MAN

Thrifty Saturn

Metal remote control holder
Calf-high socks
Luggage carrier
Wild animal prints
A durable flashlight
Popcorn maker
A blue checked sweater
A hammock
Firecrackers
A book on great geniuses of the world
Mensa membership

Luxurious Venus

Antique coins
Pheasant dinner
An electric blue parka
A psychedelic painted van
Lapis lazuli cuff links
Recessed lighting
Electric guitar
White-water rafting trip
Vintage radios
A multicolored caftan
Digital camera
Digital satellite system
Motorized scooter

Bountiful Jupiter

An electric car
A private jet
Trip to Cyprus
A house full of windows in the mountains
A private acupuncturist
A ticket on the first public moon rocket
A hot air balloon
Personal foundation
Antique firearms
A star sapphire ring
Neon sign or sculpture

AQUARIUS WOMAN

Thrifty Saturn

Tin-topped birdhouse
A weathervane
Glow in the dark phone
Christmas bubble lights
Plaid blouse
Lucite paperweight in the shape of a star
Amaretto
Blue popcorn
Celtic sea salt
Full spectrum light bulbs
Subscription to *The Utne Reader* magazine
Lava lamp

Luxurious Venus

A wishing well
Obsidian jewelry

Torchère lamps
An aquamarine ring
Silk patchwork quilt
A violet kimono
A pet toucan
Trip to Salzburg, Austria
A silver lamé dress
A blue Vespa
Collection of hats

Bountiful Jupiter

A string of black pearls
A cell phone for anywhere in the world
Fire opal jewelry
A ski chalet
Trip throughout Russia
A magic lamp that grants three wishes
A Calder mobile
A Kirilian photograph of his or her aura
An octagon-shaped home
Digital home lighting

AQUARIAN BOYS AND TEENS

A huge TV set
Puzzles
H. G. Wells' *The Time Machine*
A short wave radio
Remote control airplane
Home planetarium
Purple hair dye
Stuffed toy penguin
Pocket weather radio

Constellation T-shirt
A telescope
Trip to a rodeo
Blue sweater
A mynah bird
A hand buzzer
An old-fashioned telegraph machine
Book on how to play the electric guitar
A ventriloquist's dummy
Photographs of rainbows
Lightning-shaped tattoo
A large bubble blower
Robot
A gyroscope
Brightly colored socks
Video of *2001: A Space Odyssey*
Glow in the dark stars
Trip to the planetarium

AQUARIUS GIRLS AND TEENS

Stuffed unicorn
Any unicorn posters or symbols
An ankle bracelet
Inflatable furniture
Moving to Mozart video
Glittery eye makeup
Feather boa
Electric-pink pajamas
Photo of a shooting star
Rainbow print sheets
Green hair dye
Book on how to draw caricatures

Constellation watch
Ankle socks
Jacinth jewelry
A canary
A tie-dyed shirt
Bag of fortune cookies
A pen pal
A mood ring
A go-cart
A plaid skirt
A pop-up tent
Book on astrology for kids
Hair jewelry
Glow in the dark ceiling stars
Trip to the planetarium

Pisces
February 19–March 20

PISCES
A Mutable Yin Sign

SYMBOL:	Two Fish tied together
RULING PLANET:	Neptune
ELEMENT:	Water
BODY PART:	The feet
FAVORED POSSESSIONS:	An aquarium, comfortable shoes, and a yin/yang symbol
COMMUNICATION STYLE:	Emotional and vague
HOME STYLE:	Fantasy oriented, neat and cocoon-like
COLORS AND METAL:	Purple, sea green, black/white, platinum
FOOD, PLANTS, FLOWERS:	Fish, cucumber, chicory, pussy willows, and orchids
PARTNERSHIP STYLE:	Devoted and imaginative
RULING PASSION:	To feel comfortable in the world
PHILOSOPHY:	Love is the greatest motivator
GEMSTONES:	Amethyst, sapphire
WISHES OR GOALS:	To incorporate intuition in everyday life
UNCONSCIOUS DESIRE:	To retreat from harsh realities
FOR GIFT-GIVING, KEEP IN MIND:	Pisces cares more for expressions of love than material objects.

Character Traits and Symbols

Pisces, the last sign of the zodiac, is the most receptive and potentially spiritual sign. Pisces' symbol is two fish tied together, and in many depictions, one fish is above the water and in the light of day, while the other is in the depths of the ocean. Thus part of every Piscean is unfathomable. Pisces' imagination and artistic abilities come from these depths. Emotional sensitivity is the hallmark of all water signs, but in Pisces it is especially acute. Pisces needs more rest and down time than other signs. Reality is too abrasive to Pisces and they need to recoup their energies to keep in top form.

We say in astrology that Pisces marks the end of the personality and the beginning of the return to spirit. The intangible, feeling world is Pisces' home rather than the everyday material world. Pisces quickly picks up on the vibrations of a room or a group of people. They have a natural sixth sense and may not be able to articulate why they feel the way they do. Lest you think that the best gift for Pisces would be a one-way ticket to the mountaintop for contemplation, give your Pisces an amethyst crystal or a cuddly puppy and you will see a happy person. I've noticed that most Pisces are comfortable in their own material world as long as there is order, color, and tidiness. Many Pisceans are excellent organizers and, sometimes, clean freaks. I think this is their way of creating a world on dry land that feels secure. It is easy, when the ocean of feelings is so huge, to get lost or overwhelmed.

When astrologers first began observing the stars, there were only seven planets and Pisces was ruled by Jupiter, the greater benefic planet. The bountiful generosity of Jupiter and the desire to help humanity is definitely part of Piscean nature. In 1846, the planet Neptune was discovered and astrologers assigned this watery planet to Pisces' rulership. Subsequent observation has confirmed that Neptune is a gaseous planet of fog and mists. Fog and mist is a good metaphor for some Pisceans. Pisces could easily enjoy a world where there is a constant pink glow from drugs or alcohol. It is a tendency that many have to watch out for.

Neptune is also a planet that symbolizes spiritual visions. In ancient mythology Neptune (the Greek Poseidon) was the god of the sea. The symbol for the planet Neptune in astrology is similar to the trident Poseidon carried. Navigation in ancient times was a precarious adventure and the changeable nature of Poseidon or Neptune held the fate of sailors in his hands. Would they reach dry land or be cast adrift? You may ponder these questions when considering your Pisces friends and lovers. There is something elusive and absentminded about these people that can be very endearing, yet you may always feel you don't quite understand something about them. The feeling Pisces understands more than any other sign is compassion. They are willing to "walk a mile in the other person's moccasins" before saying a word of judgment. Pisces can be self-centered but when they are called on to serve others or to be a good friend they listen well and will try to help.

Pisces, along with Gemini, Virgo and Sagittarius, is a mutable sign. The mutable signs mark the change as we move from one season to another. The mutable signs are flexible and go with the flow. Pisces in particular is flexible and noncommittal. Unlike Libra, who has difficulty making decisions, a Pisces says "whatever" and really doesn't care much about many issues or ideas that get other people very upset. Their decisions about what they choose to do creep up on them and then they realize, "Oh, so that's what I am going to do." Pisces could use a little toughening in this department because it may be too easy to float along rather than guide the ship.

Typically, Pisces has trouble with time schedules. They rarely wear watches and have to be in the rhythm of something before they can get to appointments on time. Planning a schedule that depends on clock time goes against their nature. If your Pisces swims a little slowly, consider giving them an alarm clock they can carry with them. That way they can set it and be alerted that they have to leave to go wherever.

Pisces rules the feet and all Pisceans crave comfortable and attractive shoes. Many times these people have foot difficulties. A foot massage, pedicure, foot cream, or purple socks are perfect gifts for both men and women. If you want to butter up your Pisces spouse, sit on the sofa and rub his or her feet. The current fashion for toe rings would please Pisces. Choose a silver ring and you will delight your Pisces friend. Ballet slippers for lounging around the house, fluffy slippers, or soft jazz shoes for men would be considerate gifts for Pisces. Shoe shining seems to have gone out of fashion, but I know a Pisces doctor who received a complete shoe shine kit for Christmas and on Saturday mornings he loved to shine all his shoes.

Both male and female Pisces will appreciate any gift involving relaxation that gives them permission to retreat. Gift certificates for a spa day, short golf vacation, massage, facial, or foot rub are all ways for Pisces to melt into a fantasy world and replenish their energy. Listening to music with headphones is a great way of taking a mental holiday. Perhaps the best gift anyone could give a Pisces would be a hot tub. A good soak after work and the world will be kinder and easier for them to deal with.

Pisces will pick up all the vibes around them and no matter what gift you choose, if your gifts express your good feelings, they will always be treasured.

Colors and Flowers

The major colors for Pisces are lavender, greens and shades of blue. If you think of all the varieties of the sea from azure tropical waters, the sea-green of coastal waters and the deep blue of the ocean, you will have a good idea of the colors that Pisces like. I have also noticed that the fish like black-and-white combinations. One Pisces lady I know only wears black-and-white outfits. She also has an aquarium with many angel fish, a delicate tropical fish that has alternating black stripes on a white background.

Flowers are very important to Pisces. Many of this sign tend beautiful gardens and seem to have a knack for creating an outdoor environment that seems tame and natural at the same time. A pond with water lilies and goldfish darting about would be a great source of pleasure to Pisces. The lotus flower as well as orchids are Piscean flowers. Probably the nicest Piscean flowers are violets. Pisces loves houseplants. Cut flowers in a simple vase are a better gift than arranged flowers.

Metals, Gems, and Materials

Gems that delight Pisces are alexandrite, amethyst, coral, and aquamarine. Pisces rarely collects jewelry for its value. They may like a piece for sentimental reasons or for its beauty. Elizabeth Taylor, a beautiful Pisces who has fabulous jewelry, frequently said that one of her great pleasures was to take her jewels out and play with them in the light. Considering she has a few diamonds over ten carats, it must have been a great game! Pisces prefers platinum or white gold to yellow gold.

The materials that appeal to Pisces are soft and cuddly. Chenille is ideal. Veils and diaphanous materials give Pisces a sense of mystery. For everyday wear, wool is Pisces-ruled.

Food, Herbs, Tastes, and Scents

Herbs and herbal remedies suit Pisces' sensitivity. The sign has a low tolerance for alcohol, drugs, and strong medicines. Pisces should try out all medicines before taking a large dose. Herbs such as golden seal, echinacea, and valerian are good medicinal herbs if Pisces' system gets out of whack. Spicy food with turmeric and ginger can help with sluggish digestion. Rhubarb is a peculiar taste but very healthful especially in the spring. More than one Pisces I know makes a great rhubarb pie and seems to enjoy it more than other signs. Pisces prefer eating fish rather than meat. Salty tastes such as anchovies and caviar could be particular favorites. All sea vegetables and kelp are ruled by Pisces and this is a good source of vitamins and minerals. Pisces can get lazy about watching their diet.

Complex scents are good choices for Pisces. Rose de mai, lavender, and clematis are excellent choices. Pisces is very sensitive to heavy perfumes.

Travel

Pisceans love to travel and like to be comfortable wherever they go. Being in nature is a great tonic to their nervous system but they do not like to rough it. A palatial tent with Oriental rugs, and luxurious divans would be great . . . and if there could be a hookup for the VCR, CD player, etc., so much the better. Destinations traditionally associated with Pisces are southern Asia, Egypt, Portugal, and Seville, Spain. One Piscean friend said that her cruise down the Nile was the highlight of her life. For some odd reason, the Sahara is ruled by Pisces. Although the desert is the absolute opposite environment of the ocean, I think the expanse of dunes and sand is in keeping with Pisces' understanding of the infinite. Travel gifts should include a journal/scrapbook so Pisces can keep track of where they have been.

Sports

Pisces usually do well in sports because they have a natural sense of rhythm. They may gravitate to water sports but will also enjoy horseback riding as well as aerobic dance. T'ai chi and other softer martial arts would be wonderful to keep Pisces' energies flowing. There is a new dance/aerobic exercise called NIA that is done with bare feet. This would especially appeal to Pisces. Gifts for your sports-minded Pisces should begin with flashy footwear. An array of colored T-shirts might be another thoughtful present. Pisces is not overly concerned with what they wear but they do love color.

Piscean sports personalities abound and in a variety of surprising fields. Darryl Strawberry, for all his health and drug difficulties, was a great ballplayer. The great Jackie Joyner-Kersee, three-time Olympic medal winner, was born March 3. She established numerous records in the long jump and was rumored to have very strong feet. Dr. J., or Julius Erving, one of the great slam-dunk basketball players, was a

Pisces. My Sagittarius sports consultant said, "That guy was so light on his feet, he could fly." Last, two of the most successful race car drivers, Mario Andretti and Roger Penske, are Pisces. Both these men had long careers with few accidents.

Intellectual and Artistic Interests

Most Pisces enjoy music and many have musical talents themselves. Singing in a choir or just in the shower is a wonderful release of emotion and helps to keep a good sense of rhythm. Poetry is ruled by Pisces and sometimes your Piscean may wake up and say, "I dreamed a poem." Urge them to write it down. Visually, Pisces can create a fantastic world of color and light. Gifts such as colored tissue paper, watercolors, or colored beads will enhance Pisces' innate artistic abilities. All dance is a Pisces activity. It is a great way for Pisces to express emotion and keep in shape.

Pisces are also usually interested in occult matters. The great clairvoyant Edgar Cayce was Pisces. His biography is fascinating reading and there is an entire center for studying his works in Virginia Beach, Virginia. Pisces needs to keep in touch with the mystical part of life but it is equally important to know that planet Earth is where we live. A small word of caution: If your Pisces is interested in occult studies, make sure the information is positive and supportive. Pisces can absorb negative vibes easily and needs to learn psychic self-defense.

Romance

Pisces are in love with romance. They are not idealists like Libra but their feelings are so tender that the entire dance of courtship, or dating, is like a flower unfolding. Their compassion is immense, and if you are the object of a Pisces' desire, prepare to be wooed, flattered, and put on a pedestal. Pisceans love sensation and feeling soft materials against their bodies. The only thing to keep in mind is that dreams do not always pay the rent. Pisces men or women who emphasize the dreaminess of this sign can really have difficulties with the hard realities of making a living. Nevertheless, if that necessary evil has been mastered, Pisces is a tender, considerate mate and will listen to and share real feelings. Gifts for your Pisces amour should be romantic and fanciful. A pink lampshade for evenings á deux or a soft robe or luscious scents would be perfect.

Well-Known Pisces

With all this talk of Piscean imagination and sensitivity you may be surprised to learn that the man who changed the entire basis of twentieth-century physics and our notion of the way light and matter coexist was a Pisces. Albert Einstein was born in March. His theory of relativity has permeated all knowledge and led even nonscientists to consider the relationship of the observer to any observed phenomena. Einstein "discovered" his theory in a very Piscean way: He imagined what would happen if he rode a beam of light and looked at an adjacent beam.

Although his discovery indirectly led to nuclear fission and atomic weapons, he was mindful of a religious sense of order in the world and as a scientist his work was to interpret and uncover that order. He was a profoundly spiritual man. There have been countless movies, biographies, operas and plays inspired by Einstein's life. I have seen posters of his shaggy, kindly face hanging on the walls of many Pisces' homes and offices.

An equally monumental Piscean was Michelangelo. Michelangelo was a sculptor, architect, and painter. A visit to the Sistine Chapel would be a wonderful trip for anyone, but Pisces may feel more connected than other people to Michelangelo's soaring vision of humanity. The image of God's finger reaching out to Adam has been commercialized for movies, telephone commercials, and other marketing devices but the image and feeling it engenders remains unsullied and true. We are all trying to reach out and connect to one another. There are some early sculptures of Michelangelo's in the Uffizi Gallery in Florence called *The Prisoners*; these figures in marble were statues that he never finished because he said they wouldn't "emerge" from the stone. Give your artistically inclined Pisces a book of Michelangelo's works or a reproduction. He or she will enjoy meditating on it and it may inspire them toward their own artistic creations.

Photography is frequently a Piscean hobby. The great photographer Ansel Adams was a Pisces. His black-and-white photos are beautiful studies and make natural landscapes look otherworldly. In the fine arts, Renoir, Botticelli, and Mondrian are all fish.

The blending of colors and light in Renoir's paintings seems to me to accord with Pisces' awareness of subtle distinctions.

The list of Piscean musicians and composers is long. *The Four Seasons* by Vivaldi, Ravel's *Bolero*, and Chopin's *Nocturnes* are wonderful compositions by Piscean composers. The great operatic tenor Enrico Caruso was a Pisces, and today one of the prima donnas of the opera world, Kiri Te Kanawa, is also a Pisces. In popular music the most famous Pisces is the late George Harrison of the Beatles. Harrison was probably the most reflective personality of the group and it was at his urging that the Beatles began to meditate and traveled to India. Other noteworthy Pisces musicians are the late Kurt Cobain, Queen Latifah, Jon Bon Jovi, Sly Stone, and Nat King Cole.

In literature, the best gift to give a young Pisces would be the Dr. Seuss books. The blend of rhyme and silliness captures a sense of humor that I associate with Pisces. Poetry is a Piscean art and two wonderful American poets, Robert Lowell and Edna St. Vincent Millay, are wonderful examples of lyricism and meaning. A collection of their poems would be a great gift. For novels, there is no better gift than either Victor Hugo's *Les Miserables* or *The Hunchback of Notre Dame*. Both these books have been made into videos and there are many classic comic book versions. Hugo was intimately involved with the social injustices of the day, as illustrated by the gripping story in *Les Miserables* of the prisoner Jean Valjean. Interestingly, Pisces rules prisons and places of retreat.

In showbiz, a number of Pisces have made their

mark. Probably the most famous Piscean is Elizabeth Taylor. Filmmaking is ruled by Neptune and Pisces film performers have an intimacy with the camera that other performers must work to achieve. I believe it is attributable to the subtle levels of feelings that Pisces can communicate. Elizabeth Taylor married Scorpio Richard Burton twice. Burton was a consummate stage actor, and when he first worked with Taylor on *Cleopatra*, he complained bitterly to the director that she was not doing anything. Then he saw the film dailies and was stupefied at the way her every nuance translated to film. Other Pisces actresses are Joanne Woodward, Glenn Close, and Liza Minnelli. In addition to winning an Academy Award for the film *Three Faces of Eve*, Joanne Woodward is an accomplished ballet dancer and has aided the careers of many young choreographers. Current Piscean actresses are Drew Barrymore and Jennifer Love Hewitt.

Piscean male performers are very prominent in the entertainment business. And some of these fish are very funny people. Two giants of comedy are Jerry Lewis and Jackie Gleason. Jerry Lewis' movie *The Nutty Professor*, which he wrote, directed, and starred in, is a classic. On film or on stage, Jerry Lewis is a master showman. He also illustrates the Piscean compassion in his work fund-raising for muscular dystrophy. Jackie Gleason performed on film and in the classic fifties television comedy *The Honeymooners*. He hated to rehearse. If you watch the show, you will notice a spontaneity and hilarity that only comes from live performances and improvisation. A boxed set of these classic comedies would be a great gift.

Another wonderful Pisces comedian is Billy Crystal. If you haven't seen his movie *Mr. Saturday Night*, rent the video and watch it with your Pisces friend. Dramatic actors include Sidney Poitier, Bruce Willis, Peter Fonda, Michael Caine, and Rex Harrison.

Pisces: Response to Celebrations and Occasions

BIRTHDAY

Pisceans enjoy celebrating their birthday on the exact day. I think this is because sometimes they can be vague about time and planning a celebration on the proper day gives them a definite sense of their specialness. A party is a nice idea, but Pisces can suffer a loss of energy if the group of people is too large. There can be too many vibrations for Pisces to feel comfortable. Plan a quiet event and you will bring out the best in the fish. If you create a fantasy atmosphere with ribbons and streamers your Pisces will love it. A gift that particularly expresses affection will be most appreciated.

CHRISTMAS/HANUKAH

The spirit of giving is something Pisces has all year round. They may abhor the commercialization of these holidays and decide to take their Christmas money up to the "neediest cases fund." They will enjoy family and friends getting together and appreciate the affection of those near and dear to them.

ENGAGEMENT/MARRIAGE

A Pisces woman will appreciate the style that her fiancé uses when proposing. It doesn't have to be fancy and she won't care if he spends a lot of money on a ring. A Pisces man may totally surprise his intended by casually suggesting that they tie the knot. The important part for both Pisceans is that their feelings will be respected and the home they build together will be safe. The wedding may be outdoors at the seashore or in a small church. Gifts for the kitchen, such as cookware or a gourmet delivery service, may be a good choice. Sometimes Pisces forgets to eat.

NEW BABY

Piscean parents are well equipped to handle the emotional needs of a newborn. It will be, however, a strain on their physical energies to keep up with the feedings, etc. The best gift may be a rocking chair. It will soothe baby and parent. CDs of lullabies and perhaps an environmental tape of falling rain or ocean sounds is a great idea. A Pisces baby usually is placid and deeply interested in his or her surroundings. These children react very positively to the music.

ANNIVERSARY

One Pisces couple I know celebrated their fifth anniversary by unplugging the phone, and going on vacation in their home. They had a great time. More social fish may consider going on a short trip or having an overnight in a hotel. Change of atmosphere gives Pisces new feelings and insights. The sign is intrinsically romantic and will want to plan their day to include a luxurious meal with soft lighting and mood music.

VALENTINE'S DAY

Pisces' compassion is such that he or she is apt to remember all the people who don't get valentines on this day and try to redress the problem. For his or her particular sweetie chocolate, flowers, and a special dinner at a restaurant will be a way of keeping the love flames burning. And if you forget the day, your Pisces will probably not seethe in anger.

MOTHER'S DAY

Pisces moms could be like the old woman in the shoe who had so many children she didn't know what to do. Not all Pisces mothers have a lot of children but they have so much involvement with their kids that even one fills up their time and their heart. On Mother's Day a Pisces mom may be content to cook and have people over. If you go out let her choose the place, and for a surprise put a present under her pillow. She will appreciate discovering it before she goes off to dreamland.

FATHER'S DAY

A Pisces dad enjoys his kids because they express their feelings easily and he likes to share feelings. Adults sometimes have closed off their emotions. Pisces dads keep young by sharing the part of themselves that remains a child. A relaxing day at the beach, fishing, or eating a lobster dinner may be the best way to celebrate Father's Day. Best gift choices could be a Parcheesi game, comfortable slippers, or a new tropical fish for the aquarium.

GRADUATION

Launching oneself into the working world is not always a happy event for Pisces. They may swim around a good deal before settling on a profession or work. Encourage them to stay grounded with books about turning dreams into reality. One that comes to mind is *What Color Is Your Parachute?* If your Pisces is going to work in an office give a gift that will enhance their environment, such as a bonsai plant or a small fountain.

THANK-YOU PRESENT

If you call your Pisces friend and explain that you couldn't give them a thank-you gift for the wonderful dinner they gave two weeks ago, you will get lots of sympathy and no recriminations. If you send a present of a case of oranges from Florida because you know your friend likes them, you will receive such thanks that you will forget that you were the one thanking your Piscean friend in the first place. Pisces knows how to be grateful and likes to have gratitude expressed to them in turn.

ANYTIME PRESENT

Giving a Pisces presents is always a treat because they are more used to giving than receiving. Picking up the check is one nice gesture or giving them something for the sick kitten or the friend in need is a thoughtful way to express your affection. A little dessert special will also bring a smile to a Pisces face. Another wonderful idea is a gift certificate for a foot massage.

Pisces Gift Suggestions

PISCES MAN

Thrifty Saturn

Yellow socks
A fishbowl
Blue-green shirt
Seltzer bottles
Beer from around the world
A portable CD player
Cigars
Yearlong pass to the movies
Gourmet coffees
Diving mask
Bathing suit
Snorkeling gear

Luxurious Venus

A water bed
Scuba equipment or lessons
Digital movie camera
Book on interpreting dreams
Fly-fishing rod
Salt water fishing trip
A canoe
A harem (better move to Utah)!
Ice cream maker
Maroon sweater
A meerschaum pipe
Imported cigarettes
A ship in a bottle
Black-and-white photographic prints

Bountiful Jupiter

A private lagoon
A personal string quartet
A hot air balloon
Limousine with shaded windows
Field of oil wells
Computer navigation equipment
An island home
A three-masted schooner
A large aquarium
A garden maze
Buddha sculpture
Tibetan wall hangings

PISCES WOMAN

Thrifty Saturn

Angora mittens
Zen alarm clock (awakes with gentle chimes)
Teas from around the world
A white teapot
Natural sponges
Fishnet stockings
A bonsai tree
Lavender sheets
Pumice stone
Orchids
Rose de mai soap
Bubble bath
Dead Sea salts
Pastel drawing crayons
Book of poetry

Luxurious Venus

Purple leather boots with low heels
Reproduction of Tiffany stained glass windows
Wave-shaped candlesticks
Tourmaline necklace
A water lily pond
Shoes, shoes, and more shoes
Moonstone earrings
A fur muff
Collection of great poetry
A psychic reading
A tin-framed mirror
Angel ornaments

Bountiful Jupiter

A full-length mink coat
A water garden
Home on the beach
A summer in Normandy, France
Platinum and diamond jewelry
A personal psychic
Circular swimming pool
An elegant home fountain
Peridot jewelry
A cruise around the world

PISCES BOYS AND TEENS

Goldfish
A hydro rocket
A bubble blower
A stuffed toy whale
A dolphin watch

Sea-green blankets or comforter
A fisherman's hat
A surfboard
An aquarium
Book of Grimm's fairy tales
A toy windmill
Book on religions of the world
A small dog
Model sailboat kit
Motorized boat
Jet ski
Interactive tarot card computer game
A synthesizer
A harp
A snow globe
Boat neck shirt
Jaws and *Jaws II* (the videos)
Digital camera
Skipping stones
Purple hair dye
Rollerblades

PISCES GIRLS AND TEENS

Amethyst toe ring
A telescope
A yoga video
Thai silk throw pillows (green and blue)
A miniature tea set
Purple boots
A lava lamp
Pool goggles
Pool membership

Many cats and dogs
Bright blue galoshes
Circle pins
Beryl jewelry
Gold filigree earrings
A stuffed toy pink flamingo
A guardian angel pin
A pansy print comforter
Dance leotards
Ballet shoes
A chenille sweater
Many-colored turtleneck sweaters
A rubber plant
A cello
A spray perfume bottle
A full theatrical makeup kit
Ice skates
A kitten
Ballet slippers